ARTIFICIAL INTELLIGENCE
FOR COMPLETE BEGINNERS

A Step-by-Step Guide to Building Intelligent Systems with Python

RICHARD D. CROWLEY

Table of Contents

Part I

Laying the Foundation

CHAPTER 1

Welcome to the World of AI: Demystifying Intelligence

"Welcome to the World of AI: Demystifying Intelligence" marks the beginning of our exploration into artificial intelligence. This initial chapter aims to break down the complexities of AI, providing a clear understanding of its definition, historical development, and the different types of AI. We'll examine the fundamental concepts of algorithms, data, and learning, while also addressing the crucial ethical considerations that come with AI's growing societal impact. Finally, we'll guide you through setting up your Python environment, providing the practical foundation needed to embark on your AI journey.

1.1 What is Artificial Intelligence? Defining the Scope

At its core, Artificial Intelligence (AI) is the science and engineering of creating intelligent machines, particularly intelligent computer programs.[12] But what does "intelligence" truly mean in this context? It's a question that has captivated philosophers, scientists, and engineers for centuries.

- **A Multifaceted Definition:**
    - AI involves the ability of a machine to perform tasks that typically require human intelligence.[3] These tasks include:
        - Reasoning: Drawing logical inferences and solving problems.[4]
        - Learning: Acquiring knowledge and improving performance over time.[5]

- ■ Perception: Interpreting sensory inputs, such as images and sounds.[6]
- ■ Language understanding: Comprehending and generating human language.[7]
- ■ Problem-solving: finding solutions to complex issues.[8]

- ○
- ○ Essentially, AI aims to replicate or simulate human cognitive functions in machines.[9]

- **The Importance of Algorithms and Data:**
  - ○ AI systems rely heavily on algorithms, which are sets of instructions that enable machines to process information and make decisions.[10]
  - ○ Data is the fuel that powers AI.[11] Machine learning, a key subset of AI, involves training

algorithms on vast amounts of data to enable them to recognize patterns and make predictions.[12]

- **The Scope of AI:**
  - AI is a broad field encompassing various subfields, including:
    - Machine learning
    - Deep learning
    - Natural language processing (NLP)
    - Computer vision
    - Robotics[13]
  - It is important to understand that AI is not a singular technology, but a collection of technologies.[14]

1.2 The Historical Journey: From Concept to Reality

The concept of artificial intelligence has a rich and fascinating history, spanning centuries and encompassing contributions from diverse fields.[15]

- **Early Concepts:**
  - The idea of artificial beings dates back to ancient myths and legends.[16]
  - In the 17th and 18th centuries, mechanical automata were created, demonstrating the potential for machines to mimic human actions.[17]
- **The Birth of AI:**
  - The term "artificial intelligence" was coined in 1956 at the Dartmouth Workshop, considered the founding event of AI as a field.[18]
  - Early AI research focused on symbolic reasoning and problem-solving, with the development of programs that could play chess and solve mathematical problems.[19]

- **The AI Winters:**
  - AI research experienced periods of decline, known as "AI winters," due to limitations in computing power and a lack of practical applications.[20]
  - However, advancements in hardware and software, along with the availability of large datasets, have led to a resurgence of AI in recent years.[21]
- **Modern AI:**
  - Today, AI is transforming various industries, from healthcare and finance to transportation and entertainment.[22]
  - Deep learning, a subset of machine learning, has achieved remarkable success in areas such as image recognition and natural language processing.[23]

1.3 Types of AI: Narrow, General, and Superintelligence

AI is often categorized into three main types, based on its capabilities and level of intelligence.[24]

- **Narrow AI (ANI):**
  - Also known as "weak AI," ANI is designed to perform a specific task or set of tasks.[25]
  - Most AI systems in use today are ANI, such as virtual assistants, recommendation systems, and image recognition software.
  - ANI excels in its designated area but lacks the ability to generalize its intelligence to other tasks.[26]
- **Artificial General Intelligence (AGI):**
  - Also known as "strong AI," AGI refers to AI systems with human-level intelligence.[27]

- AGI would be capable of performing any intellectual task that a human being can do.[28]
- AGI is still a theoretical concept, and no AGI systems currently exist.

- **Artificial Superintelligence (ASI):**
  - ASI is a hypothetical form of AI that surpasses human intelligence in all aspects.[29]
  - ASI would be capable of solving problems and making discoveries that are beyond the capacity of human minds.[30]
  - The potential implications of ASI are a subject of much debate and speculation.

Key Takeaways:

- AI is a rapidly evolving field with the potential to revolutionize various aspects of our lives.[31]
- Understanding the history and types of AI is essential for comprehending its current state and future directions.
- It is very important to consider the ethical implications of AI development.

1.4 Core Concepts: Algorithms, Data, and Learning

At the heart of AI lies a triad of fundamental concepts: algorithms, data, and learning.[1] Understanding how these elements interact is crucial to grasping the essence of AI.

- **Algorithms: The Blueprint of Intelligence**
  - An algorithm is a well-defined sequence of instructions that a computer follows to solve a

problem or perform a task.[2] In AI, algorithms are the "brains" behind intelligent systems.[3]

- Different types of algorithms exist, each suited for specific tasks.[4] For example:
  - **Search algorithms:** Used for finding solutions in a vast search space (e.g., pathfinding in a map).
  - **Sorting algorithms:** Arranging data in a specific order (e.g., sorting search results).[5]
  - **Machine learning algorithms:** Enabling systems to learn from data and improve their performance over time (e.g., linear regression, decision trees).[6]

- The efficiency and effectiveness of an AI system heavily depend on the choice and design of its algorithms.

- **Data: The Fuel for Learning**
  - Data is the raw material that powers AI systems.[7] Without data, algorithms would be unable to learn and make accurate predictions.
  - The quality and quantity of data are critical factors in AI development.[8] Large, diverse, and well-labeled datasets are essential for training robust and reliable models.[9]
  - Data can take various forms, including:
    - **Structured data:** Organized in rows and columns (e.g., databases, spreadsheets).[10]
    - **Unstructured data:** Not organized in a predefined manner (e.g., text, images, audio).[11]

- Data preprocessing, which involves cleaning, transforming, and preparing data for analysis, is a crucial step in the AI pipeline.[12]
- **Learning: The Process of Acquiring Knowledge**
  - Learning is the ability of an AI system to improve its performance over time by acquiring knowledge from data.[13]
  - Machine learning, a key subset of AI, focuses on developing algorithms that can learn from data without explicit programming.[14]
  - Different types of machine learning exist, including:
    - **Supervised learning:** Learning from labeled data (e.g., classifying emails as spam or not spam).[15]

- **Unsupervised learning:** Discovering patterns in unlabeled data (e.g., clustering customers based on their purchasing behavior).[16]
- **Reinforcement learning:** Learning through trial and error by interacting with an environment (e.g., training a robot to navigate a maze).[17]

○ The learning process involves training algorithms on data, evaluating their performance, and iteratively refining them to improve their accuracy and efficiency.[18]

1.5 Ethical Considerations: The Impact of AI on Society

As AI becomes increasingly integrated into our lives, it is essential to address the ethical implications of its development and deployment.

- **Bias and Fairness:**
    - AI systems can inherit biases from the data they are trained on, leading to unfair or discriminatory outcomes.[19]
    - It is crucial to ensure that AI systems are trained on diverse and representative datasets to mitigate bias.[20]
    - Developing fairness-aware algorithms and evaluation metrics is essential for building ethical AI systems.[21]
- **Privacy and Security:**

- AI systems often collect and process vast amounts of personal data, raising concerns about privacy and security.[22]
- It is essential to implement robust data protection measures and ensure that AI systems comply with relevant privacy regulations.[23]
- Developing privacy-preserving AI techniques is crucial for safeguarding sensitive information.[24]

- **Job Displacement:**
  - AI automation has the potential to displace workers in various industries, leading to job losses and economic disruption.[25]
  - It is important to consider the social and economic implications of AI automation and develop strategies to mitigate its negative impacts.

- Retraining and upskilling programs are needed to help workers adapt to the changing job market.
- **Autonomous Weapons:**
  - The development of autonomous weapons systems raises serious ethical concerns about the potential for unintended consequences and the loss of human control.[26]
  - International regulations and ethical guidelines are needed to govern the development and use of autonomous weapons.[27]
- **Transparency and Accountability:**
  - AI systems can be complex and opaque, making it difficult to understand how they arrive at their decisions.[28][29]
  - It is essential to develop explainable AI (XAI) techniques that can provide insights into

the decision-making process of AI systems.[30]

- Accountability frameworks are needed to ensure that AI systems are used responsibly and ethically.[31]

1.6 Setting Up Your Python Environment for AI

To begin your journey into AI, you'll need to set up a Python environment with the necessary libraries and tools.[32]

- **Python Installation:**
    - Download and install the latest version of Python from the official Python website (python.org).[33]
    - Ensure that you add Python to your system's PATH environment variable.

- **Virtual Environments:**
  - Create a virtual environment to isolate your AI projects and prevent conflicts between different library versions.[34]
  - Use the venv module or conda to create virtual environments.
- **Package Management:**
  - Use pip to install and manage Python packages.
  - Install essential AI libraries, such as:
    - NumPy: For numerical computing.
    - Pandas: For data manipulation and analysis.
    - Scikit-learn: For machine learning algorithms.
    - TensorFlow or PyTorch: For deep learning.
    - Matplotlib and Seaborn: For data visualization.
- **Integrated Development Environment (IDE):**

- Choose an IDE to write and run your Python code. Popular options include:
    - VS Code
    - PyCharm
    - Jupyter Notebooks/Lab.[35]
- **Testing your installation:**
    - After the installation of the libraries, write small python programs that utilize the imported libraries. This will verify that the installation was successfully.

By understanding these core concepts, ethical considerations, and setting up your environment, you'll be well-prepared to explore the exciting world of Artificial Intelligence.

CHAPTER 2

Python Essentials for AI: Your Programming Toolkit

"Python Essentials for AI: Your Programming Toolkit" lays the groundwork for using Python in AI development. This chapter covers fundamental Python concepts: variables, data types, control flow (loops and conditionals), and essential data structures (lists, dictionaries, tuples, and sets). It then progresses to building reusable code with functions and modules, and introduces NumPy for numerical computing and Pandas for data manipulation and analysis. Mastering these tools is crucial for any aspiring AI practitioner, providing the necessary foundation to build and deploy intelligent systems.

Python's simplicity and versatility make it the language of choice for AI development.

This chapter will equip you with the fundamental Python skills necessary to build intelligent systems.

2.1 Python Basics: Variables, Data Types, and Operators

Understanding the building blocks of Python is crucial before venturing into more complex AI concepts.

- **Variables:**
    - Variables are used to store data in a program. In Python, you don't need to declare the data type of a variable explicitly; Python infers it based on the assigned value.
    - Variable names must follow certain rules: they can contain letters, numbers, and underscores, but they cannot start with a number.

- Example:
- Python

```
age = 30
name = "Alice"
is_student = True
```

- ○
- ○

- **Data Types:**
  - Python offers various built-in data types to represent different kinds of data:
    - **Integers (int):** Whole numbers (e.g., 10, -5, 0).
    - **Floating-point numbers (float):** Numbers with decimal points (e.g., 3.14, -2.5).

- **Strings (str):** Sequences of characters (e.g., "Hello", "Python").
- **Booleans (bool):** Represent truth values (True or False).
  - Python is a dynamically typed language, meaning that the data type of a variable can change during program execution.
- **Operators:**
  - Operators perform operations on variables and values:
    - **Arithmetic operators:** +, -, *, /, %, ** (exponentiation), // (floor division).
    - **Comparison operators:** ==, !=, >, <, >=, <=.
    - **Logical operators:** and, or, not.
    - **Assignment operators:** =, +=, -=, *=, /=, etc.

- Understanding operator precedence is essential for writing correct expressions.

2.2 Control Flow: Loops and Conditional Statements

Control flow statements allow you to control the order in which code is executed.

- **Conditional Statements (if, elif, else):**
    - Conditional statements execute different blocks of code based on whether certain conditions are true or false.
    - The if statement checks a condition and executes a block of code if the condition is true.
    - The elif (else if) statement checks additional conditions if

the previous if or elif conditions are false.

- The else statement executes a block of code if all previous conditions are false.
- Example:
- Python

```
score = 85
if score >= 90:
    print("A")
elif score >= 80:
    print("B")
else:
    print("C")
```

-
-

- **Loops (for, while):**

- Loops allow you to repeat a block of code multiple times.
- for **loop:** Iterates over a sequence (e.g., a list, tuple, or string) or other iterable object.
- Python

```
for i in range(5):
    print(i)
```

-
-
- while **loop:** Executes a block of code as long as a condition is true.
- Python

```
count = 0
```

```
while count < 5:
    print(count)
    count += 1
```

- ○
- ○
- ○ break and continue statements can be used to control the flow of loops.

2.3 Data Structures: Lists, Dictionaries, and Tuples

Data structures are essential for organizing and managing data in a program.

- **Lists:**
  - ○ Lists are ordered, mutable (changeable) sequences of elements.

- Elements in a list can be of different data types.
- Lists are created using square brackets [].
- Example:
- Python

```
my_list = [1, "apple", 3.14, True]
my_list.append("banana") #adds to the end of the list.
print(my_list[0]) #prints the first item in the list.
```

-
-

- **Dictionaries:**
  - Dictionaries are unordered collections of key-value pairs.

- Keys must be unique and immutable (e.g., strings, numbers, or tuples).
- Values can be of any data type.
- Dictionaries are created using curly braces {}.
- Example:
- Python

```
my_dict = {"name": "Bob", "age": 25, "city": "New York"}
print(my_dict["name"])
```

-
-

- **Tuples:**
  - Tuples are ordered, immutable sequences of elements.
  - Tuples are created using parentheses ().

- Tuples are similar to lists, but they cannot be modified after creation.
- Example:
- Python

```
my_tuple = (1, "hello", 3.14)
print(my_tuple[1])
```

-
-
- **Set:**
    - Sets are unordered collections of unique elements.
    - Sets are created using curly braces {}, or the set() function.
    - Example:
    - Python

```
my_set = {1,2,3,4,4,5}
print(my_set) #output {1, 2, 3, 4, 5} notice
the duplicate 4 was removed.
```

o

o

These fundamental Python concepts provide a solid foundation for your AI programming journey. By mastering these essentials, you'll be well-equipped to tackle more complex AI algorithms and build intelligent systems.

2.4 Functions and Modules: Building Reusable Code

As your AI projects grow in complexity, organizing your code becomes paramount.

Functions and modules provide the means to create reusable and maintainable code.[1]

- **Functions:**
    - Functions are blocks of organized, reusable code that perform a specific task.[2]
    - They promote code modularity and reduce redundancy.
    - Functions are defined using the def keyword, followed by the function name, parentheses (), and a colon :.
    - Functions can take input parameters (arguments) and return output values.[3]
    - Example:
    - Python

```
def calculate_area(length, width):
    """Calculates the area of a rectangle."""
    area = length * width
```

```
    return area

rectangle_area = calculate_area(5, 10)
print(rectangle_area)
```

- ○
- ○
- ○ Docstrings (documentation strings) are used to describe the purpose and usage of a function.[4]
- **Modules:**
  - ○ Modules are Python files containing functions, classes, and variables.[5]
  - ○ They allow you to organize and reuse code across multiple projects.[6]
  - ○ Modules are imported using the import statement.
  - ○ Python has a vast standard library of built-in modules, and

you can also create your own custom modules.[7]
- ○ Example:
- ○ Python

```python
# my_module.py
def greet(name):
    return f"Hello, {name}!"

# main.py
import my_module

message = my_module.greet("Charlie")
print(message)

import math
print(math.sqrt(16))
```

- ○
- ○

- Using from module import function you can import specific functions from a module.
- Using import module as alias you can give a module a shorter alias.

2.5 Introduction to NumPy: Numerical Computing in Python

NumPy (Numerical Python) is a fundamental library for numerical computing in Python.[8] It provides powerful tools for working with arrays and matrices, essential for AI tasks.[9]

- **NumPy Arrays:**
  - NumPy arrays are multidimensional arrays that can store elements of the same data type.[10]

- They are much more efficient than Python lists for numerical operations.[11]
- NumPy arrays are created using the numpy.array() function.
- Example:
- Python

```
import numpy as np

my_array = np.array([1, 2, 3, 4, 5])
print(my_array)

matrix = np.array([[1, 2, 3], [4, 5, 6]])
print(matrix)
```

-
-

- **Array Operations:**

- NumPy provides a wide range of functions for performing mathematical operations on arrays, including:
    - Element-wise operations (addition, subtraction, multiplication, division).[12]
    - Matrix operations (dot product, transpose).
    - Statistical operations (mean, standard deviation).[13]
    - Linear algebra functions.

- **Array Indexing and Slicing:**
  - NumPy arrays support powerful indexing and slicing techniques, similar to Python lists.[14]
  - You can access individual elements or subarrays using indices and slices.

- **Broadcasting:**
  - NumPy's broadcasting feature allows you to perform operations on arrays of different

shapes, making it easy to perform element-wise operations on arrays with compatible dimensions.[15]

2.6 Introduction to Pandas: Data Manipulation and Analysis

Pandas is a powerful library for data manipulation and analysis in Python.[16] It provides data structures and functions for working with[17] structured data, such as tables and time series.[18]

- **Pandas[19] DataFrames:**
    - Pandas DataFrames are two-dimensional tables that can store data of different types.[20]
    - They are similar to spreadsheets or SQL tables.
    - DataFrames are created from various data sources, such as

CSV files, Excel files, and Python dictionaries.[21]
- ○ Example:
-

import pandas as pd

```
data = {"name": ["Alice", "Bob",
"Charlie"], "age": [25, 30, 35], "city": ["New
York", "London", "Paris"]}
df = pd.DataFrame(data)
print(df)

df = pd.read_csv("my_data.csv")
```
```

- **Data Selection and Filtering:**
  - ○ Pandas provides powerful tools for selecting and filtering data in DataFrames.[22]
```

- You can select columns, rows, or specific elements based on conditions.
- **Data Cleaning and Transformation:**
  - Pandas offers functions for cleaning and transforming data, such as:
    - Handling missing values.
    - Removing duplicates.
    - Renaming columns.
    - Applying functions to columns.
- **Data Aggregation and Grouping:**
  - Pandas allows you to group data and perform aggregate calculations, such as sums, averages, and counts.[23]
- **Data Visualization:**
  - Pandas integrates well with Matplotlib and Seaborn for creating visualizations of data.[24]

These Python essentials—functions, modules, NumPy, and Pandas—form the foundation upon which you'll build your AI applications. By mastering these tools, you'll be well-equipped to handle the data-intensive tasks that are central to AI development.

CHAPTER 3

The Power of Data: Understanding and Preparing Your Datasets

Data is the lifeblood of AI. Without high-quality, relevant data, even the most sophisticated algorithms will falter.[1] This chapter explores the essential steps involved in acquiring, cleaning, and understanding your datasets.

3.1 Data Collection: Sources and Methods

The journey of building an AI model begins with gathering the right data.[2] The quality and relevance of your data directly impact the performance and reliability of your model.[3]

- **Diverse Data Sources:**
  - **Public Datasets:** Many organizations and institutions provide open-access datasets, such as those from government agencies (e.g., data.gov), research institutions, and Kaggle.[4] These datasets can be valuable resources for experimentation and learning.
  - **Web Scraping:** Extracting data from websites can be a powerful method, particularly for text and image data.[5] However, it's crucial to respect website terms of service and legal regulations regarding data usage.
  - **APIs (Application Programming Interfaces):** APIs allow you to access data from online services in a structured and programmatic manner.[6] Many social media

platforms, financial services, and other online platforms provide APIs for data access.[7]

- **Databases:** Organizations often store data in databases.[8] Accessing these databases may require specific permissions and credentials.[9]

- **Sensors and IoT Devices:** In domains like environmental monitoring and industrial automation, data can be collected from sensors and IoT devices.[10]

- **Surveys and Experiments:** For specific research questions, you may need to conduct surveys or experiments to collect custom data.

- **Data Collection Methods:**
  - **Automated Collection:** Using scripts and programs to automate data retrieval from various sources.[11]

o **Manual Collection:** Gathering data through manual processes, such as surveys, interviews, or observations.[12]
o **Data Acquisition Platforms:** Utilizing platforms and services that specialize in data collection and aggregation.

3.2 Data Cleaning: Handling Missing and Inconsistent Data

Raw data is rarely perfect. It often contains errors, inconsistencies, and missing values that can negatively impact model performance.[13] Data cleaning is the process of addressing these issues to ensure data quality.[14]

- **Identifying Missing Data:**

- Use techniques like isnull() and notnull() in Pandas to identify missing values in your dataset.
- Visualize missing data patterns using heatmaps or other visualization methods.
- **Handling Missing Data:**
  - **Deletion:** Removing rows or columns with missing values. This approach should be used cautiously, as it can lead to data loss.
  - **Imputation:** Replacing missing values with estimated values.[15] Common imputation methods include:
    - Mean imputation: Replacing missing values with the[16] mean of the column.[17]
    - Median imputation: Replacing missing values with the median of the column.[18]

- Mode imputation: Replacing missing values with the mode of the column.[19]
- Forward fill or backward fill: filling missing values with the previous or next valid value.[20]
- Using algorithms to predict the missing values.

    ○

    ○ **Creating Indicator Variables:** Adding a binary variable that indicates whether a value was missing.

- **Addressing Inconsistent Data:**
    ○ **Data Type Conversion:** Ensuring that data types are consistent and appropriate (e.g., converting strings to numbers).
    ○ **Standardization and Normalization:** Scaling numerical data to a common range to prevent features with

larger scales from dominating the model.[21]

- o **Handling Outliers:** Identifying and addressing extreme values that can distort the data distribution.[22]
- o **Removing Duplicates:** Eliminating duplicate records to ensure data integrity.[23]
- o **Correcting Typos and Errors:** Identifying and correcting errors in text data.

3.3 Data Exploration: Visualizing and Summarizing Data

Before building a model, it's essential to understand the characteristics of your data. Data exploration involves summarizing and visualizing data to gain insights and identify patterns.[24]

- **Summary Statistics:**
  - Calculate descriptive statistics, such as mean, median, standard deviation, and quartiles, to summarize the distribution of numerical data.[25]
  - Use Pandas' describe() function to generate summary statistics.
- **Data Visualization:**
  - **Histograms:** Visualize the distribution of numerical data.[26]
  - **Scatter Plots:** Explore the relationship between two numerical variables.[27]
  - **Box Plots:** Identify outliers and visualize the distribution of data.[28]
  - **Bar Charts:** Visualize the distribution of categorical data.[29]
  - **Heatmaps:** Visualize the correlation between variables.[30]
- **Correlation Analysis:**
  - Calculate correlation coefficients to quantify the strength and

direction of linear relationships between numerical variables.

- ○ Use Pandas' corr() function to calculate correlation matrices.
- **Data Profiling:**
  - ○ Generate reports that summarize the characteristics of your data, including data types, missing values, and distributions.

By mastering data collection, cleaning, and exploration, you'll be well-equipped to prepare your datasets for building effective AI models.

3.4   Feature   Engineering: Creating Meaningful Inputs

Feature engineering is the art and science of creating new features from existing data to improve the performance of machine learning models.[1] It involves transforming raw data into[2] meaningful inputs that capture the underlying patterns and relationships.[3]

- **Understanding Feature Engineering:**
    - The goal is to create features that are relevant to the prediction task and that capture the essential information in the data.
    - Feature engineering requires domain knowledge and an understanding of the data.[4]
    - It is an iterative process that involves experimentation and evaluation.[5]
- **Feature Engineering Techniques:**
    - **Creating Polynomial Features:** Generating polynomial terms from existing features to capture non-linear relationships.[6]

- Binning **Numerical Features:** Converting continuous numerical features into discrete categorical features by grouping values into bins.[7]
- **Encoding Categorical Features:** Transforming categorical features into numerical representations that machine learning models can understand.[8] Common encoding methods include:
  - **One-Hot Encoding:** Creating binary columns for each category.[9]
  - **Label Encoding:** Assigning a unique[10] numerical label to each category.[11]
  - **Ordinal Encoding:** Assigning numerical labels based on the order or ranking of categories.
-

- **Feature Scaling and Normalization:** Scaling numerical features to a common range to prevent features with larger scales from dominating the model.[12] Techniques include:
  - **Standardization:** Scaling features to have zero mean and unit variance.[13]
  - **Normalization:** Scaling features to a specific[14] range, such as [0, 1].[15]
-
- **Feature Extraction from Text Data:** Extracting meaningful features from text data, such as:
  - **Bag-of-Words (BoW):** Representing text as a collection of words and their frequencies.
  - **Term Frequency-Inverse**

Document Frequency (TF-IDF): Weighting words based on their importance in a document and across a corpus.[16]

- **Word Embeddings:** Representing words as dense vectors that capture semantic relationships.[17]

○ **Feature Extraction from Image Data:** Extracting features from images, such as:

- **Pixel Values:** Using raw pixel values as features.

- **Edge Detection:** Identifying edges and boundaries in images.[18]

- **Texture Analysis:** Capturing texture patterns in images.

- **Convolutional Neural Network (CNN) Features:** Using features learned by CNNs.

- Creating Interaction
  Features: Combining existing
  features to create new features
  that capture interactions
  between them.[19]
- Time-Series Features:
  Extracting features from
  time-series data, such as:
    - Lag Features: Using
      previous values as
      features.
    - Rolling Statistics:
      Calculating rolling
      averages and standard
      deviations.[20]
    - Seasonality Features:
      Capturing seasonal
      patterns in the data.[21]

3.5 Data Splitting: Training, Validation, and Testing Sets

To evaluate the performance of a machine learning model and prevent overfitting, it's essential to split the data into training, validation, and testing sets.[22]

- **Training Set:**
  - The training set is used to train the model.[23]
  - It contains the majority of the data.
- **Validation Set:**
  - The validation set is used to evaluate the model's performance during training and to tune hyperparameters.[24]
  - It helps to prevent overfitting by providing an independent measure of the model's performance.
- **Testing Set:**

- The testing set is used to evaluate the final performance of the trained model.[25]
- It provides an unbiased estimate of the model's generalization ability.
- **Splitting Techniques:**
  - **Random Splitting:** Randomly dividing the data into training, validation, and testing sets.
  - **Stratified Splitting:** Ensuring that the class distribution is preserved in each split. This is particularly important for classification tasks with imbalanced datasets.
  - **Time-Series Splitting:** Splitting time-series data based on time order to prevent future data from leaking into the training set.[26]
- **Scikit-learn's** train_test_split() **Function:**

- Scikit-learn provides the train_test_split() function for splitting data into training and testing sets.
- You can specify the test size, random state, and stratification parameters.

3.6 Introduction to Scikit-learn: Building Machine Learning Models

Scikit-learn is a powerful and widely used Python library for machine learning.[27] It provides a comprehensive set of tools for building and evaluating machine learning models.

- **Scikit-learn's Features:**
    1. **Simple and Consistent API:** Scikit-learn's API is designed to

be user-friendly and consistent across different algorithms.[28]

2. **Wide Range of Algorithms:** Scikit-learn provides a wide range of machine learning algorithms for classification, regression, clustering, and dimensionality reduction.[2930]

3. **Data Preprocessing Tools:** Scikit-learn offers tools for data preprocessing, such as feature scaling, encoding, and imputation.[31]

4. **Model Evaluation Metrics:** Scikit-learn provides metrics for evaluating the performance of machine learning models.[32]

5. **Model Selection and Hyperparameter Tuning:** Scikit-learn offers tools for selecting the best model and tuning its hyperparameters.[33]

- **Building a Machine Learning Model with Scikit-learn:**

1. **Import the necessary libraries.**
2. **Load and prepare the data.**
3. **Split the data into training and testing sets.**
4. **Choose a machine learning algorithm.**
5. **Create an instance of the model.**
6. **Train the model on the training data.**
7. **Make predictions on the testing data.**
8. **Evaluate the model's performance.**

- **Example:**
- Python

```
from sklearn.model_selection import train_test_split
from sklearn.linear_model import LinearRegression
```

```python
from           sklearn.metrics          import
mean_squared_error

# Load and prepare data (example)
X = [[1], [2], [3], [4], [5]]
y = [2, 4, 5, 4, 5]

X_train,   X_test,   y_train,   y_test   =
train_test_split(X,      y,      test_size=0.2,
random_state=42)

model = LinearRegression()
model.fit(X_train, y_train)

y_pred = model.predict(X_test)

mse = mean_squared_error(y_test, y_pred)
print(f"Mean Squared Error: {mse}")
```

-
-

By mastering feature engineering, data splitting, and Scikit-learn, you'll be well-equipped to build and evaluate effective machine learning models.

Part II

Core Machine Learning Algorithms

CHAPTER 4

Supervised Learning: Learning from Labeled Data - Regression

Supervised learning is a fundamental branch of machine learning where algorithms learn from labeled data.[1] Regression, a key technique within supervised learning, focuses on predicting continuous values.[2]

4.1 Introduction to Supervised Learning

Supervised learning is characterized by the presence of labeled data, where each input data point is associated with a corresponding output or target.[3]

- **The Concept of Labeled Data:**

- Labeled data consists of input features (independent variables) and corresponding target values (dependent variables).[4]
- The goal of supervised learning is to learn a mapping function that can accurately predict the target values for new, unseen input data.[5]
- Examples of labeled data include:
  - House prices (target) associated with features like square footage, number of bedrooms, and location.
  - Email spam/not spam (target) associated with features like email content and sender information.[6]
- **Types of Supervised Learning:**
  - **Regression:** Predicting continuous target values (e.g., house prices, stock prices).[7]

- **Classification:** Predicting categorical target values (e.g., spam/not spam, image classification).[8]
- **The Learning Process:**
  - The supervised learning algorithm learns from the training data by adjusting its internal parameters to minimize the difference between[9] predicted and actual target values.[10]
  - The learning process involves:
    - Training the model on the labeled data.
    - Evaluating the model's performance on a separate validation or testing set.
    - Iteratively refining the model to improve its accuracy.
- **Applications of Supervised Learning:**

- Supervised learning is widely used in various applications, including:
  - Predictive analytics.[11]
  - Image recognition.
  - Natural language processing.
  - Fraud detection.

4.2 Linear Regression: Predicting Continuous Values

Linear regression is a fundamental and widely used technique for predicting continuous target values based on a linear relationship with input features.[12]

- **The Linear Relationship:**
  - Linear regression assumes that there is a linear relationship

between the input features and the target variable.[13]

- o The relationship can be represented by a linear equation:
    - y = mx + b (for a single input feature), where:
        - y is the predicted target value.
        - x is the input feature.
        - m is the slope of the line (coefficient).
        - b is the y-intercept.
    - For multiple input features the equation expands to.
        - $y = b + m_1x_1 + m_2x_2 + \ldots + m_nx_n$

- **The Goal of Linear Regression:**
    - o The goal is to find the best-fitting line (or hyperplane in higher dimensions) that minimizes the difference between the predicted[14] and actual target values.

- This is typically achieved by minimizing the sum of squared errors (least squares method).[15]

- **The Least Squares Method:**
  - The least squares method finds the optimal values for the coefficients (m and b) by minimizing the sum of the squared differences between the predicted and actual target values.[16]
  - This can be done using analytical methods or iterative optimization algorithms.

- **Assumptions of Linear Regression:**
  - Linearity: A linear relationship exists between the input features and the target variable.
  - Independence: The errors (residuals) are independent of each other.
  - Homoscedasticity: The errors have constant variance.[17]

- Normality: The errors are normally distributed.
- No Multicollinearity: The independant variables are not strongly correlated with each other.[18]
- **Implementation in Python (Scikit-learn):**
  - Scikit-learn provides the LinearRegression class for building linear regression models.
  - The process involves:
    - Creating an instance of the LinearRegression class.
    - Training the model using the fit() method.
    - Making predictions using the predict() method.
    - Evaluating the model using metrics like Mean Squared Error (MSE), or R-squared.[19]

Python

```python
from sklearn.linear_model import LinearRegression
from sklearn.model_selection import train_test_split
from sklearn.metrics import mean_squared_error

# Example data (replace with your data)
X = [[1], [2], [3], [4], [5]]  # Input features
y = [2, 4, 5, 4, 5]  # Target values

# Split data into training and testing sets
X_train, X_test, y_train, y_test = train_test_split(X, y, test_size=0.2, random_state=42)

# Create and train the linear regression model
model = LinearRegression()
model.fit(X_train, y_train)

# Make predictions
y_pred = model.predict(X_test)
```

```
# Evaluate the model
    mse = mean_squared_error(y_test,
y_pred)
    print(f"Mean Squared Error: {mse}")
```

Linear regression is a powerful and interpretable technique for predicting continuous values.[20] Its simplicity and effectiveness make it a valuable tool in the AI practitioner's toolkit.

4.3 Polynomial Regression: Capturing Non-Linear Relationships

While linear regression is effective for linear relationships, many real-world datasets exhibit nonlinear patterns.[1] Polynomial regression extends linear regression to capture these non-linear relationships.[2]

- **The Concept of Polynomial Regression:**
  - Polynomial regression fits a polynomial curve to the data, rather than a straight line.[3]
  - The polynomial equation takes the form:
    - $y = b + m_1x + m_2x^2 + m_3x^3 + ... + m_nx^n$
    - Where n is the degree of the polynomial.
  - By increasing the degree of the polynomial, the model can fit more complex curves.[4]
- **Creating Polynomial Features:**
  - To perform polynomial regression, you need to create polynomial features from the original input features.[5]
  - Scikit-learn's PolynomialFeatures class can be used to generate polynomial features.
  - Example:

from sklearn.preprocessing import PolynomialFeatures

import numpy as np

```
X = np.array([[1], [2], [3], [4]])
poly = PolynomialFeatures(degree=2)
X_poly = poly.fit_transform(X)
print(X_poly)
```

- **Fitting the Polynomial Regression Model:**
  - Once you have created the polynomial features, you can fit a linear regression model to them.
  - This is because the polynomial equation is still linear in terms of the coefficients (m1, m2, m3, etc.).
- **Choosing the Degree of the Polynomial:**

- The degree of the polynomial is a hyperparameter that needs to be tuned.[6]
- A low degree may underfit the data, while a high degree may overfit the data.[7]
- Cross-validation can be used to select the optimal degree.

- **Overfitting and Underfitting:**
  - **Underfitting:** Occurs when the model is too simple to capture the underlying patterns in the data (e.g., fitting a linear model to a non-linear dataset).
  - **Overfitting:** Occurs when the model is too complex and fits the noise in the data, leading to poor generalization on unseen data.
  - It is crucial to find a balance between underfitting and overfitting.

4.4 Evaluating Regression Models: Metrics and Techniques

Evaluating the performance of a regression model is crucial to assess its accuracy and reliability.[8]

- **Common Evaluation Metrics:**
  - **Mean Squared Error (MSE):** The average of the squared differences between the predicted and actual target values.[9] Lower values indicate better performance.
    - MSE = (1/n) * Σ(y_actual - y_predicted)^2
  -
  - **Root Mean Squared Error (RMSE):** The square root of the MSE.[10] It provides an error metric in the same units as the target variable.
    - RMSE = √MSE

-
- **Mean Absolute Error (MAE):** The average of the absolute differences between the predicted and actual target values.[11] It is less sensitive to outliers than MSE.
    - MAE = $(1/n) * \Sigma|y\_actual - y\_predicted|$
-
- **R-squared (Coefficient of Determination):** Measures the proportion of the variance in the target variable that is predictable from the[12] input features.[13] Higher values (closer to 1) indicate better performance.
    - R^2 = 1 - (SS_res / SS_tot)
    - SS_res is the sum of squared residuals.
    - SS_tot is the total sum of squares.

o

- **Evaluation Techniques:**
  - **Train-Test Split:** Splitting the data into training and testing sets to evaluate the model's generalization ability.
  - **Cross-Validation:** Dividing the data into multiple folds and training and evaluating the model on different combinations of folds. This provides a more robust estimate of the model's performance.
  - **Residual Analysis:** Plotting the residuals (differences between predicted and actual values) to check for patterns or violations of assumptions.[14]
  - **Learning Curves:** Plotting the model's performance on the training and validation sets as a function of the training set size.[15][16] This helps to identify overfitting or underfitting.

4.5 Practical Implementation: Building Regression Models in Python

Let's demonstrate how to build and evaluate regression models in Python using Scikit-learn.

Python

```python
import numpy as np
import matplotlib.pyplot as plt
from sklearn.linear_model import LinearRegression
from sklearn.preprocessing import PolynomialFeatures
from sklearn.model_selection import train_test_split
from sklearn.metrics import mean_squared_error, r2_score

# Example data (replace with your data)
X = np.array([[1], [2], [3], [4], [5], [6], [7], [8], [9], [10]])
```

```python
y = np.array([2, 5, 10, 17, 26, 37, 50, 65, 82,
101])  # Non-linear relationship

# Split data into training and testing sets
X_train, X_test, y_train, y_test =
train_test_split(X, y, test_size=0.2,
random_state=42)

# Polynomial Regression (degree=2)
poly = PolynomialFeatures(degree=2)
X_poly_train = poly.fit_transform(X_train)
X_poly_test = poly.transform(X_test)

model_poly = LinearRegression()
model_poly.fit(X_poly_train, y_train)
y_poly_pred =
model_poly.predict(X_poly_test)

# Linear Regression
model_linear = LinearRegression()
model_linear.fit(X_train, y_train)
y_linear_pred =
model_linear.predict(X_test)
```

```python
# Evaluate models
mse_poly = mean_squared_error(y_test, y_poly_pred)
r2_poly = r2_score(y_test, y_poly_pred)
mse_linear = mean_squared_error(y_test, y_linear_pred)
r2_linear = r2_score(y_test, y_linear_pred)

print(f"Polynomial Regression MSE: {mse_poly}, R2: {r2_poly}")
print(f"Linear Regression MSE: {mse_linear}, R2: {r2_linear}")

# Visualize results
plt.scatter(X_test, y_test, color='black')
plt.plot(X_test, y_poly_pred, color='red', label='Polynomial Regression')
plt.plot(X_test, y_linear_pred, color='blue', label='Linear Regression')
plt.legend()
plt.show()
```

By understanding polynomial regression, evaluation metrics, and practical implementation, you'll be able to build and evaluate effective regression models for a wide range of applications.

CHAPTER 5

Supervised Learning: Learning from Labeled Data- Classification

Classification is a core area of supervised learning where the goal is to predict categorical labels or classes.[1] This chapter will cover the fundamentals of classification and explore two popular algorithms: logistic regression and decision trees.

5.1 Introduction to Classification: Categorical Predictions

Classification tasks involve predicting which category or class a data point belongs to, based on its features.[2]

- **Categorical Targets:**

- Classification deals with target variables that are discrete and represent categories.[3]
- Examples include:
    - Email spam detection (spam or not spam).[4]
    - Image classification (identifying objects in images).[5]
    - Medical diagnosis (disease or no disease).

- **The Classification Process:**
    - The classification algorithm learns from labeled data, where each data point is associated with a specific class.[6]
    - The goal is to build a model that can accurately assign new, unseen data points to their correct classes.

- **Types of Classification:**
    - **Binary Classification:** Predicting between two classes (e.g., yes/no, true/false).[7]

- Multiclass Classification: Predicting between more than two classes (e.g., classifying different types of animals).[8]
- Multilabel Classification: Assigning multiple labels to a single data point (e.g., tagging images with multiple objects).[9]
- **Key Concepts:**
  - Features: The input variables used to make predictions.[10]
  - Classes/Labels: The categorical outcomes being predicted.
  - Decision Boundary: The boundary that separates different classes in the feature space.[11]

5.2 Logistic Regression: Binary Classification

Logistic regression is a powerful and widely used algorithm for binary classification.[12] Despite its name, it's a classification algorithm, not a regression algorithm.

- **The Logistic Function (Sigmoid):**
    - Logistic regression uses the sigmoid function to transform the linear combination of input features into a probability between 0 and 1.[13]
    - The sigmoid function is defined as:
        - $\sigma(z) = 1 / (1 + e^{\wedge}(-z))$
        - Where z is the linear combination of the inputs.
    - This function outputs a S shaped curve, that restricts the output to the range of 0 to 1.

- **Binary Classification with Probabilities:**
  - Logistic regression predicts the probability that a data point belongs to a particular class.[14]
  - If the probability is greater than a certain threshold (typically 0.5), the data point is assigned to that class.[15]
  - If the probability is below the threshold, it is assigned to the other class.
- **The Decision Boundary:**
  - Logistic regression creates a linear decision boundary that separates the two classes.[16]
  - The decision boundary is defined by the equation:
    - $z = b + m_1x_1 + m_2x_2 + \ldots + m_nx_n = 0$
- **Training Logistic Regression:**
  - Logistic regression is trained using maximum likelihood estimation, which aims to find

the parameters that maximize the likelihood of observing the training data.[17]

- ○ Gradient descent is commonly used to optimize the parameters.[18]
- **Implementation in Python (Scikit-learn):**
  - ○ Scikit-learn provides the LogisticRegression class for building logistic regression models.
  - ○ Example:
- Python

```
from sklearn.linear_model import LogisticRegression
from sklearn.model_selection import train_test_split
from sklearn.metrics import accuracy_score

# Example data (replace with your data)
X = [[1, 2], [2, 3], [3, 4], [5, 6], [6, 7], [7, 8]]
```

```python
y = [0, 0, 0, 1, 1, 1]

X_train, X_test, y_train, y_test = train_test_split(X, y, test_size=0.2, random_state=42)

model = LogisticRegression()
model.fit(X_train, y_train)

y_pred = model.predict(X_test)

accuracy = accuracy_score(y_test, y_pred)
print(f"Accuracy: {accuracy}")
```

-
-

5.3 Decision Trees: Understanding Decision-Making Processes

Decision trees are powerful and interpretable algorithms that model decision-making processes using a tree-like structure.[19]

- **Tree Structure:**
    - A decision tree consists of nodes and branches.[20]
    - Each node represents a feature, and each branch represents a decision rule.[21]
    - The leaves of the tree represent the predicted classes.[22]
- **Decision Rules:**
    - Decision trees make decisions by following a series of decision rules based on the values of the input features.[23]

- At each node, the algorithm selects the feature and threshold that best splits the data into different classes.[24]
- **Information Gain and Gini Impurity:**
  - Decision trees use metrics like information gain and Gini impurity to select the best features and thresholds for splitting the data.[25]
  - These metrics measure the reduction in impurity or increase in information after a split.
- **Advantages of Decision Trees:**
  - Interpretable: Decision trees are easy to understand and visualize.
  - Handles both numerical and categorical features.
  - Robust to outliers.
- **Disadvantages of Decision Trees:**

- Prone to overfitting: Decision trees can become too complex and fit the noise in the data.[26]
- Sensitive to small changes in the data.

- **Implementation in Python (Scikit-learn):**
  - Scikit-learn provides the DecisionTreeClassifier class for building decision tree models.
  - Example:
- Python

```
from sklearn.tree import DecisionTreeClassifier
from sklearn.model_selection import train_test_split
from sklearn.metrics import accuracy_score

# Example data (replace with your data)
X = [[1, 2], [2, 3], [3, 4], [5, 6], [6, 7], [7, 8]]
y = [0, 0, 0, 1, 1, 1]
```

```
X_train,    X_test,    y_train,    y_test    =
train_test_split(X,    y,    test_size=0.2,
random_state=42)

model = DecisionTreeClassifier()
model.fit(X_train, y_train)

y_pred = model.predict(X_test)

accuracy = accuracy_score(y_test, y_pred)
print(f"Accuracy: {accuracy}")
```

-
-

Logistic regression and decision trees are fundamental algorithms for classification tasks.[27] Their simplicity and effectiveness make them valuable tools in the AI practitioner's arsenal.

5.4 Support Vector Machines (SVMs): Finding Optimal Boundaries

Support Vector Machines (SVMs) are powerful algorithms for classification and regression that aim to find the optimal hyperplane that separates different classes.[1]

- **The Concept of Hyperplanes:**
  - In a two-dimensional space, a hyperplane is a line that separates different classes.[2]
  - In higher dimensions, a hyperplane is a higher-dimensional surface.
  - SVMs aim to find the hyperplane that maximizes the margin between the classes.[3]
- **The Margin:**
  - The margin is the distance between the hyperplane and the

nearest data points from each class.

- ○ Maximizing the margin leads to better generalization and robustness.[4]

- **Support Vectors:**
  - ○ Support vectors are the data points that are closest to the hyperplane and determine the margin.[5]
  - ○ Only support vectors are used to define the hyperplane.[6]

- **Kernel Trick:**
  - ○ SVMs can handle non-linear classification problems using the kernel trick.[7]
  - ○ The kernel trick maps the input data into a higher-dimensional space where it becomes linearly separable.[8]
  - ○ Common kernel functions include:
    - ■ Linear kernel.
    - ■ Polynomial kernel.

- Radial basis function (RBF) kernel.[9]
- **Soft Margin and Regularization:**
  - In real-world datasets, it may not be possible to find a perfect hyperplane that separates all classes.
  - SVMs use a soft margin to allow some misclassifications and handle noisy data.[10]
  - Regularization is used to control the trade-off between maximizing the margin and minimizing misclassifications.[11]
- **Advantages of SVMs:**
  - Effective in high-dimensional spaces.
  - Versatile due to the kernel trick.
  - Robust to outliers.
- **Disadvantages of SVMs:**
  - Can be computationally expensive for large datasets.
  - Choosing the right kernel and parameters can be challenging.

5.5 Evaluating Classification Models: Metrics and Techniques

Evaluating the performance of a classification model is crucial to assess its accuracy and reliability.

- **Common Evaluation Metrics:**
  - **Accuracy:** The proportion of correctly classified data points.
    - Accuracy = (Number of correct predictions) / (Total number of predictions)
  - **Precision:** The proportion of correctly predicted positive cases out of all predicted positive cases.[12]
    - Precision = True Positives / (True Positives + False Positives)
  -

- **Recall (Sensitivity):** The proportion of correctly predicted positive cases out of all actual positive cases.[13]
  - Recall = True Positives / (True Positives + False Negatives)
-
- **F1-Score:** The harmonic mean of precision and recall.
  - F1-Score = 2 * (Precision * Recall) / (Precision + Recall)
- **Confusion Matrix:** A table that summarizes the performance of a classification model by showing the number of true positives, true negatives, false positives, and false negatives.[1415]
- **Area Under the ROC Curve (AUC-ROC):** Measures the ability of a model to distinguish between different classes.[16]

- ROC curve plots the true positive rate against the false positive rate at various threshold settings.[17]
- AUC represents the area under the ROC curve.[1819]

  ○

- **Evaluation Techniques:**
  - **Train-Test Split:** Splitting the data into training and testing sets to evaluate the model's generalization ability.
  - **Cross-Validation:** Dividing the data into multiple folds and training and evaluating the model on different combinations of folds.[20]
  - **Stratified Cross-Validation:** Ensuring that the class distribution is preserved in each fold. This is particularly important for imbalanced datasets.

- **Choosing the Right Metrics:**
  - The choice of evaluation metrics depends on the specific problem and the relative importance of different types of errors.
  - For imbalanced datasets, metrics like precision, recall, and F1-score are often more informative than accuracy.

5.6 Practical Implementation: Building Classification Models in Python

Let's demonstrate how to build and evaluate classification models in Python using Scikit-learn.

Python

from sklearn.model_selection import train_test_split

```
from sklearn.svm import SVC
from            sklearn.metrics         import
accuracy_score,            precision_score,
recall_score, f1_score, confusion_matrix
import matplotlib.pyplot as plt
import seaborn as sns

# Example data (replace with your data)
X = [[1, 2], [2, 3], [3, 4], [5, 6], [6, 7], [7, 8]]
y = [0, 0, 0, 1, 1, 1]

# Split data into training and testing sets
X_train,   X_test,   y_train,   y_test   =
train_test_split(X,     y,     test_size=0.2,
random_state=42)

# Create and train the SVM model
model = SVC(kernel='linear')   # You can
change the kernel
model.fit(X_train, y_train)

# Make predictions
y_pred = model.predict(X_test)
```

```python
# Evaluate the model
accuracy = accuracy_score(y_test, y_pred)
precision = precision_score(y_test, y_pred)
recall = recall_score(y_test, y_pred)
f1 = f1_score(y_test, y_pred)
confusion = confusion_matrix(y_test, y_pred)

print(f"Accuracy: {accuracy}")
print(f"Precision: {precision}")
print(f"Recall: {recall}")
print(f"F1-Score: {f1}")
print(f"Confusion Matrix:\n{confusion}")

# Visualize confusion matrix
sns.heatmap(confusion, annot=True, fmt='d')
plt.xlabel('Predicted')
plt.ylabel('Actual')
plt.show()
```

By understanding SVMs, evaluation metrics, and practical implementation, you'll be well-equipped to build and evaluate effective classification models for a wide range of applications.

CHAPTER 6

Unsupervised Learning: Discovering Patterns in Unlabeled Data - Clustering

Unsupervised learning is a powerful branch of machine learning that deals with unlabeled data, aiming to discover hidden patterns and structures.[1] Clustering, a core technique within unsupervised learning, focuses on grouping similar data points together.[2]

6.1 Introduction to Unsupervised Learning

Unsupervised learning differs significantly from supervised learning in that it operates on data without explicit labels or target variables.[3]

- **The Challenge of Unlabeled Data:**
    - In unsupervised learning, the algorithm must find patterns and structures in the data without any guidance from labeled examples.[4]
    - This requires the algorithm to identify inherent relationships and similarities within the data.[5]
- **Goals of Unsupervised Learning:**
    - **Clustering:** Grouping similar data points together based on their features.
    - **Dimensionality Reduction:** Reducing the number of features while preserving[6] essential information.[7]
    - **Anomaly Detection:** Identifying data points that deviate significantly from the norm.[8]
    - **Association Rule Learning:** Discovering relationships

between variables in large datasets.

- **Applications of Unsupervised Learning:**
  - **Customer Segmentation:** Grouping customers based on their purchasing behavior or demographics.[9]
  - **Image Segmentation:** Dividing an image into meaningful regions or objects.[10]
  - **Document Clustering:** Grouping similar documents together based on their content.[11]
  - **Anomaly Detection in Fraud Detection:** Identifying unusual transactions that may indicate fraud.[12]
  - **Recommender Systems:** Suggesting products or content based on user preferences.[13]
- **Key Differences from Supervised Learning:**

- No **Target Variables:** Unsupervised learning does not involve predicting target variables.[14]
- **Pattern Discovery:** The goal is to discover hidden patterns and structures in the data.[15]
- **Evaluation Challenges:** Evaluating unsupervised learning models can be more challenging due to the lack of ground truth labels.[16]

6.2 K-Means Clustering: Grouping Similar Data Points

K-Means is a popular and widely used algorithm for clustering data points into K distinct groups.[17]

- **The Concept of Clustering:**

- Clustering aims to partition data points into clusters such that data points within the same cluster are more similar to each other than to data points in other clusters.[18]
- Similarity is typically measured using distance metrics, such as Euclidean distance.[19]

- **The K-Means Algorithm:**
  - **Initialization:** Randomly select K initial centroids (cluster centers).[20]
  - **Assignment:** Assign each data point to the nearest centroid.[21]
  - **Update:** Recalculate the centroids as the mean of the data points assigned to each cluster.[22]
  - **Iteration:** Repeat steps 2 and 3 until the centroids no longer change significantly or a maximum number of iterations is reached.[23][24]

- **Choosing the Number of Clusters (K):**
  - The number of clusters (K) is a hyperparameter that needs to be chosen.[25]
  - **Elbow Method:** Plot the within-cluster sum of squares (WCSS) as a function of K and choose the K value at the "elbow" point, where the WCSS starts to decrease less rapidly.[26]
  - **Silhouette Score:** Measures how similar a data point is to its own cluster compared to other clusters.[27]
  - **Domain Knowledge:** Using prior knowledge about the data to determine a reasonable number of clusters.
- **Distance Metrics:**
  - **Euclidean Distance:** The most common distance metric, measuring the straight-line distance between two points.

- Manhattan Distance: The sum of the absolute differences between the coordinates of two points.
- Cosine Similarity: Measures the cosine of the angle between[28] two vectors, often used for text and document clustering.[29]

- **Advantages of K-Means:**
  - Simple and easy to implement.
  - Computationally efficient for large datasets.
  - Widely used and well-understood.

- **Disadvantages of K-Means:**
  - Sensitive to the initial placement of centroids.[30]
  - Assumes that clusters are spherical and equally sized.
  - Requires the number of clusters (K) to be specified in advance.
  - Sensitive to outliers.

- **Implementation in Python (Scikit-learn):**

- Scikit-learn provides the KMeans class for building K-Means clustering models.
  - Example:
- Python

```python
from sklearn.cluster import KMeans
import numpy as np
import matplotlib.pyplot as plt

# Example data (replace with your data)
X = np.array([[1, 2], [1, 4], [1, 0], [10, 2],
[10, 4], [10, 0]])

# Create and train the K-Means model
kmeans = KMeans(n_clusters=2)  # Choose
the number of clusters
kmeans.fit(X)

# Get cluster assignments and centroids
labels = kmeans.labels_
centroids = kmeans.cluster_centers_
```

```
# Visualize the clusters
plt.scatter(X[:, 0], X[:, 1], c=labels)
plt.scatter(centroids[:, 0], centroids[:, 1],
marker='X', s=200, c='red')
plt.show()
```

-
-

K-Means clustering is a fundamental and powerful technique for discovering patterns in unlabeled data.[31] Its simplicity and effectiveness make it a valuable tool in the AI practitioner's toolkit.

6.3 Hierarchical Clustering: Building a Hierarchy of Clusters

Hierarchical clustering is a powerful technique that builds a hierarchy of clusters, allowing you to explore data at different levels of granularity.[1]

- **The Concept of Hierarchical Clustering:**
  - Unlike K-Means, which produces a flat partitioning of the data, hierarchical clustering creates a tree-like structure called a dendrogram.[2]
  - The dendrogram represents the nested relationships between clusters.[3]
  - You can choose the number of clusters by cutting the dendrogram at a desired level.[4]
- **Types of Hierarchical Clustering:**
  - **Agglomerative (Bottom-Up):** Starts with each data point as a separate cluster and iteratively merges the closest[5] clusters until all data points belong to a single cluster.[67]
  - **Divisive (Top-Down):** Starts with all data points in a single cluster and recursively splits the

clusters until each data point is in its own cluster.[89]

- **Linkage Methods:**
  - Linkage methods determine how the distance between clusters is calculated.[10]
  - Common linkage methods include:
    - **Single Linkage:** The minimum distance between any two points in the clusters.
    - **Complete Linkage:** The maximum distance between any two points in the clusters.
    - **Average Linkage:** The average distance between all pairs of points in the clusters.[11]
    - **Ward's Method:** Minimizes the variance within the clusters.[12]
- **Dendrogram Interpretation:**

- The dendrogram visually represents the clustering process.[13]
- The height of the branches indicates the distance between the merged clusters.[14]
- You can choose the number of clusters by drawing a horizontal line across the dendrogram and counting the number of branches it intersects.

- **Advantages of Hierarchical Clustering:**
  - Provides a hierarchical representation of the data.
  - Does not require the number of clusters to be specified in advance.[15]
  - Can handle different shapes and sizes of clusters.

- **Disadvantages of Hierarchical Clustering:**
  - Computationally expensive for large datasets.

- Sensitive to noise and outliers.
- Difficult[16] to interpret for high-dimensional data.

6.4 Evaluating Clustering Models: Metrics and Techniques

Evaluating the performance of clustering models is crucial to assess the quality of the clusters.

- **Intrinsic Evaluation Metrics (Without Ground Truth Labels):**
  - **Silhouette Score:** Measures how similar a data point is to its own cluster compared to other clusters.
    - Values range from -1 to 1, with higher values indicating better clustering.
  -

- Davies-Bouldin Index: Measures the average similarity between each cluster and its most similar cluster.[17]
  - Lower[18] values indicate better clustering.

-

- Calinski-Harabasz Index: Measures the ratio of between-cluster variance to within-cluster variance.[19]
  - Higher values indicate[20] better clustering.

-

- **Extrinsic Evaluation Metrics (With Ground Truth Labels):**
  - Adjusted Rand Index (ARI): Measures the similarity between the predicted clusters and the true labels, adjusted for chance.[21]
    - Values range from -1 to 1, with higher values

indicating better clustering.

-

- **Normalized Mutual Information (NMI):** Measures the mutual information between[22] the predicted clusters and the true labels, normalized by the entropy of the labels.
  - Values range from 0 to 1, with higher values indicating better clustering.

-

- **Visual Inspection:**
  - Visualizing the clusters can provide insights into the quality of the clustering.
  - Techniques like scatter plots and dendrograms can be used for visualization.[23]
- **Choosing the Right Metrics:**

- The choice of evaluation metrics depends on the availability of ground truth labels and the specific goals of the clustering task.
- Intrinsic metrics are used when ground truth labels are not available.
- Extrinsic metrics are used when ground truth labels are available.

6.5 Practical Implementation: Building Clustering Models in Python

Let's demonstrate how to build and evaluate clustering models in Python using Scikit-learn.

Python

```python
import numpy as np
import matplotlib.pyplot as plt
from sklearn.cluster import AgglomerativeClustering
from sklearn.metrics import silhouette_score, davies_bouldin_score
from scipy.cluster.hierarchy import dendrogram, linkage

# Example data (replace with your data)
X = np.array([[1, 2], [1, 4], [1, 0], [10, 2], [10, 4], [10, 0]])

# Agglomerative Clustering
agg_clustering = AgglomerativeClustering(n_clusters=2)
labels = agg_clustering.fit_predict(X)

# Silhouette Score
silhouette = silhouette_score(X, labels)
print(f"Silhouette Score: {silhouette}")

# Davies-Bouldin Index
```

```python
davies_bouldin = davies_bouldin_score(X,
labels)
print(f"Davies-Bouldin          Index:
{davies_bouldin}")

# Dendrogram
linked = linkage(X, 'ward')
dendrogram(linked,          orientation='top',
distance_sort='descending',
show_leaf_counts=True)
plt.title('Hierarchical          Clustering
Dendrogram')
plt.xlabel('Sample Index')
plt.ylabel('Cluster Distance')
plt.show()

# Visualize Clusters
plt.scatter(X[:, 0], X[:, 1], c=labels)
plt.title('Agglomerative Clustering')
plt.xlabel('Feature 1')
plt.ylabel('Feature 2')
plt.show()
```

By understanding hierarchical clustering, evaluation metrics, and practical implementation, you'll be well-equipped to discover hidden patterns and structures in unlabeled data.

CHAPTER 7

Unsupervised Learning: Discovering Patterns in Unlabeled Data - Dimensionality Reduction

Dimensionality reduction is a technique used to reduce the number of features in a dataset while preserving its essential information.[2] This is particularly important when dealing with high-dimensional data, which poses several challenges.

7.1 The Curse of Dimensionality: Challenges of High-Dimensional Data

High-dimensional data, characterized by a large number of features, presents several challenges that can negatively impact the performance of machine learning models.[3]

- **Increased Computational Complexity:**
  - As the number of features increases, the computational cost of training and evaluating models grows exponentially.
  - This can lead to longer training times and increased memory requirements.[4]
- **Sparsity of Data:**
  - In high-dimensional spaces, data points become increasingly sparse.[5]
  - This means that there are fewer data[6] points in any given region of the feature space, making it difficult to find meaningful patterns.[7]
- **Overfitting:**
  - High-dimensional data increases the risk of overfitting, where the model learns the noise in the data rather than the underlying patterns.[8]

- o This leads to poor generalization on unseen data.[9]
- **Increased Noise:**
  - o As the number of features increases, the likelihood of irrelevant or noisy features also increases.
  - o These noisy features can obscure the true signal in the data and negatively impact model performance.[10]
- **Distance Measures Become Less Meaningful:**
  - o In high-dimensional spaces, the distance between data points tends to become more uniform, making it difficult to distinguish between[11] similar and dissimilar points.
  - o This can make distance-based algorithms, such as K-Means clustering, less effective.[12]
- **Visualisation Challenges:**

o It is very hard to visualize data that has more than 3 dimensions, making it hard to understand the data.[13]

7.2 Principal Component Analysis (PCA): Reducing Data Complexity

Principal Component Analysis (PCA) is a widely used dimensionality reduction technique that transforms high-dimensional data into a lower-dimensional representation while preserving the most important[14] information.[15]

- **The Concept of Principal Components:**
  o PCA identifies the principal components of the data, which are orthogonal (uncorrelated)

linear combinations of the original features.[16]

- The principal components are ordered by the amount of variance they explain,[17] with the first principal component explaining the most variance.[18][19]

- **The Goal of PCA:**
    - The goal of PCA is to find a lower-dimensional subspace that captures the maximum variance in the data.
    - This allows you to represent the data using fewer features while preserving most of its essential information.[20]

- **The PCA Algorithm:**
    - **Standardization:** Standardize the data to have zero mean and unit variance.
    - **Covariance Matrix:** Calculate the covariance matrix of the standardized data.[21]

- ○ **Eigenvalues and Eigenvectors:** Calculate the eigenvalues and eigenvectors of the covariance matrix.
- ○ **Principal Components:** Select the top K eigenvectors corresponding to the largest eigenvalues. These eigenvectors are the principal components. 5.[22] **Transformation:** Transform the data into the lower-dimensional subspace by projecting it onto the principal components.
- **Explained Variance Ratio:**
  - ○ The explained variance ratio indicates the proportion of variance explained by each principal component.[23]
  - ○ It[24] can be used to determine the optimal number of principal components to retain.
- **Applications of PCA:**

- o **Image Compression:** Reducing the size of images while preserving their visual quality.[25]
- o **Noise Reduction:** Removing noise from data by discarding principal components with low variance.
- o **Feature Extraction:** Extracting meaningful features from high-dimensional data.[26]
- o **Data Visualization:** Visualizing high-dimensional data in a lower-dimensional space.
- **Advantages of PCA:**
  - o Reduces dimensionality while preserving most of the variance.[27]
  - o Simplifies data and reduces computational complexity.[28]
  - o Can improve the performance of machine learning models.
- **Disadvantages of PCA:**

- Can lose some information in the dimensionality reduction process.
- Principal components can be difficult to interpret.
- Sensitive to scaling of the original data.

PCA is a powerful tool for dealing with high-dimensional data.[29] By reducing the number of features, it can simplify data analysis, improve model performance, and enable visualization.[30]

7.3 t-Distributed Stochastic Neighbor Embedding (t-SNE): Visualizing High-Dimensional Data

t-Distributed Stochastic Neighbor Embedding (t-SNE) is a powerful technique specifically designed for visualizing high-dimensional data in a lower-dimensional space, typically two or three dimensions.[1]

- **The Challenge of High-Dimensional Visualization:**
    - High-dimensional data is inherently difficult to visualize directly.
    - Traditional dimensionality reduction techniques, such as PCA, may not always preserve the local structure of the data, which is crucial for visualization.
- **The Concept of t-SNE:**

- t-SNE focuses on preserving the pairwise similarities between data points in the high-dimensional space in the lower-dimensional embedding.[2]
- It models the pairwise similarities using conditional probabilities.[3]

- **The t-SNE Algorithm:**
  - **Similarity Measurement:** Measures the similarity between data points in the high-dimensional space using conditional probabilities based on Gaussian distributions.[4]
  - **Low-Dimensional Embedding:** Initializes a random low-dimensional embedding of the data points.[5]
  - **Similarity Measurement in Low Dimensions:** Measures the similarity between data points in the low-dimensional embedding using t-distributions.

- o **Optimization:** Minimizes the difference between the high-dimensional and low-dimensional similarities using gradient descent.[6]
- o **Iteration:** Repeats step 4 until convergence.
- **Advantages of t-SNE:**
  - o Effective at visualizing complex, non-linear structures in high-dimensional data.[7]
  - o Preserves local similarities between data points, making it useful for identifying clusters and patterns.[8]
- **Disadvantages of t-SNE:**
  - o Computationally expensive, especially for large datasets.[9]
  - o The results can be sensitive to the choice of hyperparameters, such as perplexity.[10]
  - o Does not preserve global distances between data points.

- Not suitable for dimensionality reduction for machine learning tasks, as it is primarily a visualization technique.
- **Perplexity:**
  - Perplexity is a hyperparameter that controls the number of nearest neighbors considered when measuring similarities.
  - It affects the trade-off between local and global structure in the embedding.[11]
  - Typical values range from 5 to 50.[12]
- **Interpretation of t-SNE Plots:**
  - Clusters in the t-SNE plot generally represent groups of similar data points.[13]
  - However, distances between clusters should not be interpreted as meaningful distances in the original high-dimensional space.

- o t-SNE is primarily a tool for exploratory data analysis and visualization.[14]

7.4 Practical Implementation: Dimensionality Reduction in Python

Let's demonstrate how to perform dimensionality reduction using PCA and t-SNE in Python with Scikit-learn.

Python

```
import numpy as np
import matplotlib.pyplot as plt
from sklearn.decomposition import PCA
from sklearn.manifold import TSNE
from sklearn.datasets import load_digits  #
Example dataset

# Load the digits dataset (high-dimensional)
```

```python
digits = load_digits()
X = digits.data
y = digits.target

# PCA Implementation
pca = PCA(n_components=2)
X_pca = pca.fit_transform(X)

# t-SNE Implementation
tsne         =         TSNE(n_components=2,
perplexity=30, random_state=42)
X_tsne = tsne.fit_transform(X)

# Visualize PCA Results
plt.figure(figsize=(12, 6))
plt.subplot(1, 2, 1)
plt.scatter(X_pca[:, 0], X_pca[:, 1], c=y,
cmap='viridis')
plt.title('PCA Visualization')
plt.xlabel('Principal Component 1')
plt.ylabel('Principal Component 2')

# Visualize t-SNE Results
plt.subplot(1, 2, 2)
```

```
plt.scatter(X_tsne[:, 0], X_tsne[:, 1], c=y,
cmap='viridis')
plt.title('t-SNE Visualization')
plt.xlabel('t-SNE Component 1')
plt.ylabel('t-SNE Component 2')

plt.show()

# Explained Variance Ratio for PCA
print(f"Explained Variance Ratio (PCA):
{pca.explained_variance_ratio_}")
```

In this example:

- We load the digits dataset, which is a high-dimensional dataset of handwritten digits.[15]
- We use PCA to reduce the dimensionality to 2 components and visualize the results.
- We use t-SNE to reduce the dimensionality to 2 components and visualize the results.

- We compare the visualizations from PCA and t-SNE.

By understanding t-SNE and its practical implementation, you'll be able to effectively visualize high-dimensional data and gain insights into its underlying structure.

Part III: Advanced AI Techniques

CHAPTER 8

Neural Networks: Building Intelligent Systems Inspired by the Brain

Neural networks, inspired by the structure and function of the human brain, are powerful machine learning models that can learn complex patterns and relationships in data.[1] This chapter will introduce the fundamental concepts of neural networks and explore the importance of activation functions.

8.1 Introduction to Neural Networks: The Building Blocks

Neural networks are composed of interconnected nodes, or neurons, organized in layers.[2] These networks learn by adjusting the connections between neurons, allowing them to process and transform information.[3]

- **The Neuron (Perceptron):**
  - The basic building block of a neural network is the neuron, also known as a perceptron.[4]
  - A neuron receives input signals, multiplies them by weights, sums them, and applies an activation function to produce an output signal.[5]
  - Mathematically, a neuron can be represented as:
    - output = activation_function(Σ(weights * inputs) + bias)
- **Layers:**
  - Neural networks are organized into layers:[6]
    - **Input Layer:** Receives the input data.[7]

- **Hidden Layers:** Perform intermediate computations.[8]
- **Output Layer:** Produces the final output.[9]
  -
  - Each layer consists of multiple neurons.[10]
  - The output of one layer serves as the input to the next layer.
- **Weights and Biases:**
  - Weights represent the strength of the connections between neurons.[11]
  - Biases are added to the weighted sum to adjust the neuron's activation threshold.[12]
  - Weights and biases are the parameters that the neural network learns during training.[13]
- **Feedforward Neural Networks:**
  - In feedforward neural networks, information flows in one direction, from the input layer to

the output layer, without any loops or cycles.[14]

- These networks are used for a wide range of tasks, including classification and regression.

- **Deep Neural Networks:**
  - Deep neural networks have multiple hidden layers, allowing them to learn more complex and abstract representations of the data.[15]
  - Deep learning refers to the training of deep neural networks.[16]

- **The Learning Process:**
  - Neural networks learn by adjusting their weights and biases to minimize the difference between the predicted and actual outputs.
  - This is typically achieved using an optimization algorithm, such as gradient descent.[17]
  - The process involves:

- **Forward Propagation:** Computing the output of the network for a given input.[18]
- **Backpropagation:** Calculating the gradients of the error function with respect to the weights and biases.[19]
- **Weight Update:** Adjusting the weights and biases based on the gradients.[20]

8.2 Activation Functions: Introducing Non-Linearity.

Activation functions are crucial components of neural networks that introduce non-linearity, enabling the network to learn complex patterns.[21]

- **The Need for Non-Linearity:**
  - Without activation functions, a neural network would simply be a linear combination of its inputs.[22]
  - Linear models are limited in their ability to learn complex relationships.[23]
  - Activation functions introduce non-linearity, allowing the network to approximate any continuous function.[24]
- **Common Activation Functions:**
  - **Sigmoid Function:**
    - Outputs values between 0 and 1.
    - Used for binary classification tasks.[25]
    - Suffers from vanishing gradient problem.
    - $\sigma(z) = 1 / (1 + e^{\wedge}(-z))$
  - **Tanh (Hyperbolic Tangent) Function:**

- Outputs values between -1 and 1.
- Similar to the sigmoid function, but centered at 0.
- Also suffers from vanishing gradient problem.[26]
- $tanh(z) = (e^{\wedge}z - e^{\wedge}(-z)) / (e^{\wedge}z + e^{\wedge}(-z))$

o **ReLU (Rectified Linear Unit) Function:**
- Outputs the input directly if it is positive, and 0 otherwise.
- Simple and computationally efficient.
- Helps to mitigate the vanishing gradient problem.
- $ReLU(z) = max(0, z)$

o **Leaky ReLU Function:**

- Similar to ReLU, but introduces a small slope for negative inputs.
- Helps to address the "dying ReLU" problem, where neurons can become inactive.
- Leaky ReLU(z) = max(αz, z) (where α is a small constant).

○ **Softmax Function:**
- Outputs a probability distribution over multiple classes.
- Used for multiclass classification tasks.[27]
- softmax(z)_i = e^(z_i) / Σ(e^(z_j))

• **Choosing Activation Functions:**
   ○ The choice of activation function depends on the specific task and the characteristics of the data.

- ReLU and its variants are commonly used in hidden layers.[28]
- Sigmoid and softmax are often used in the output layer for classification tasks.[29]

- **Vanishing Gradient Problem:**
  - The vanishing gradient problem occurs when the gradients become very small during backpropagation, making it difficult[30] to update the weights in earlier layers.[31]
  - This can hinder the training of deep neural networks.
  - ReLU and its variants help to mitigate this problem.[32]

By understanding the building blocks of neural networks and the role of activation functions, you'll be well-prepared to build and train powerful neural network models.

8.3 Forward Propagation and Backpropagation: Training Neural Networks

Training a neural network involves adjusting its weights and biases to minimize the difference between predicted and actual outputs.[1] This is achieved through forward propagation and backpropagation.[2]

- **Forward Propagation:**
    - Forward propagation is the process of computing the output of a neural network for a given input.[3]
    - It involves passing the input data through the network, layer by layer, until the output layer is reached.[4]
    - At each layer, the input is multiplied by the weights, added to the biases, and passed through the activation function.[5]

- The output of each layer serves as the input to the next layer.
- The final output of the network is compared to the actual target values to calculate the error.[6]

- **Backpropagation:**
  - Backpropagation is the process of calculating the gradients of the error function with respect to the weights and biases.[7]
  - It involves propagating the error backwards through the network, layer by layer.[8]
  - The gradients indicate how much each weight and bias contributes to the error.
  - The gradients are used to update the weights and biases in the direction that minimizes the error.[9]
  - The chain rule of calculus is used to calculate the gradients of the error function with respect to each weight and bias.

- The optimization algorithm (e.g., gradient descent) uses these gradients to update the network's parameters.[10]
- **Gradient Descent:**
  - Gradient descent is an iterative optimization algorithm that minimizes the error function by iteratively adjusting the weights and biases in the direction of the negative gradient.[11]
  - The learning rate is a hyperparameter that controls the step size of the weight and bias updates.[12]
  - A small learning rate can lead to slow convergence, while a large learning rate can lead to instability.[13]
- **Stochastic Gradient Descent (SGD):**
  - SGD is a variant of gradient descent that updates the weights and biases using a single

training example or a small batch of training examples at a time.
- ○ SGD is more efficient than batch gradient descent, which updates the weights and biases using the entire training dataset.
- ○ SGD can also help to escape local minima.[14]
- **Optimization Algorithms:**
  - ○ Other optimization algorithms, such as Adam and RMSprop, are commonly used to train neural networks.[15]
  - ○ These algorithms adapt the learning rate for each weight and bias, which can lead to faster convergence and better performance.

8.4 Building Simple Neural Networks with Keras/TensorFlow

Keras, a high-level API for building and training neural networks, is integrated with TensorFlow, a powerful open-source machine learning framework.[16]

- **Keras/TensorFlow Workflow:**
    1. **Define the Model:** Create a sequential or functional model by adding layers.
    2. **Compile the Model:** Specify the optimizer, loss function, and metrics.
    3. **Train the Model:** Fit the model to the training data using the fit() method.
    4. **Evaluate the Model:** Evaluate the model's performance on the testing data using the evaluate() method.

5. **Make Predictions:** Use the predict() method to make predictions on new data.
- **Example (Classification):**

Python

```
import tensorflow as tf
from tensorflow import keras

# Define the model
model = keras.Sequential([
                keras.layers.Dense(128,
activation='relu',
input_shape=(input_dim,)),
            keras.layers.Dense(num_classes,
activation='softmax')
    ])

# Compile the model
model.compile(optimizer='adam',
        loss='categorical_crossentropy',
        metrics=['accuracy'])
```

```python
# Train the model
model.fit(X_train, y_train, epochs=10, batch_size=32)

# Evaluate the model
loss, accuracy = model.evaluate(X_test, y_test)
print(f"Test Loss: {loss}, Test Accuracy: {accuracy}")
```

- **Example (Regression):**

Python

```python
model = keras.Sequential([
    keras.layers.Dense(128, activation='relu', input_shape=(input_dim,)),
    keras.layers.Dense(1) #one output for regression.
])
```

```
model.compile(optimizer='adam',
loss='mse')

model.fit(X_train, y_train, epochs=10,
batch_size=32)

loss = model.evaluate(X_test, y_test)
print(f"Test Loss: {loss}")
```

8.5 Evaluating Neural Network Performance

Evaluating the performance of neural networks is crucial to assess their accuracy and reliability.

- **Classification Metrics:**
  - Accuracy, precision, recall, F1-score, confusion matrix, AUC-ROC.
- **Regression Metrics:**

- Mean squared error (MSE), root mean squared error (RMSE), mean absolute error (MAE), R-squared.
- **Overfitting and Underfitting:**
  - Overfitting occurs when the model performs well on the training data but poorly on the testing data.[17]
  - Underfitting occurs when the model performs poorly on both the training and testing data.
  - Regularization techniques, such as dropout and weight decay, can help to prevent overfitting.[18]
- **Cross-Validation:**
  - Cross-validation can be used to obtain a more robust estimate of the model's performance.[19]
- **Learning Curves:**
  - Learning curves plot the model's performance on the training and validation sets as a function of the training set[20] size.[21]

- Learning curves can help to identify overfitting and underfitting.[22]
- **Hyperparameter Tuning:**
  - Hyperparameters, such as the learning rate and the number of layers, can significantly impact the performance of neural networks.[23]
  - Techniques such as grid search and random search can be used to tune hyperparameters.[24]

By mastering forward and backpropagation, Keras/TensorFlow implementation, and evaluation techniques, you'll be well-equipped to build and train effective neural network models.

CHAPTER 9

Deep Learning: Unlocking the Power of Deep Neural Networks

Deep learning, a subfield of machine learning, focuses on training deep neural networks with multiple layers.[1] This chapter will explore the architectures and applications of deep learning, with a particular emphasis on CNNs for image recognition.

9.1 Introduction to Deep Learning: Architectures and Applications

Deep learning has revolutionized various fields by enabling the development of highly accurate and powerful models.[2]

- **The Power of Deep Neural Networks:**
  - Deep neural networks, with their multiple hidden layers, can learn complex and abstract representations of data.[3]
  - This allows them to capture intricate patterns and relationships that are beyond the capabilities of shallow models.[4]
- **Key Architectures:**
  - **Convolutional Neural Networks (CNNs):** Designed for processing grid-like data, such as images and videos.[5]
  - **Recurrent Neural Networks (RNNs):** Designed for processing sequential data, such as text and time series.[6]
  - **Autoencoders:** Used for unsupervised learning tasks, such as dimensionality

reduction and anomaly detection.[7]

- ○ **Generative Adversarial Networks (GANs):**[8] Used for generating realistic data, such as images and audio.[9]
- ○ **Transformers:** Used for natural language processing and other sequence-to-sequence tasks.[10]

- **Applications of Deep Learning:**
  - ○ **Image Recognition:** Classifying and identifying objects in images.[11]
  - ○ **Natural Language Processing (NLP):** Understanding and generating human language.
  - ○ **Speech Recognition:** Converting spoken language into text.[12]
  - ○ **Autonomous Driving:** Enabling vehicles to perceive

and navigate their environment.[13]

- o **Medical Diagnosis:** Assisting in the diagnosis of diseases from medical images and data.[14]
- o **Financial Forecasting:** Predicting stock prices and other financial trends.[15]
- o **Game Playing:** Developing AI agents that can play games at a superhuman level.[16]
- **Key Advantages of Deep Learning:**
  - o **Automatic Feature Learning:** Deep learning models can automatically learn relevant features from raw data, eliminating the need for manual feature engineering.[17][18]
  - o **High Accuracy:** Deep learning models have achieved state-of-the-art results in various tasks.[19]

- ○ **Scalability:** Deep learning models can scale to large datasets and complex problems.[20]
- **Key Challenges of Deep Learning:**
  - ○ **Data Requirements:** Deep learning models typically require large amounts of labeled data for training.[21]
  - ○ **Computational Cost:** Training deep learning models can be computationally expensive and time-consuming.[22]
  - ○ **Interpretability:** Deep learning models can be difficult to interpret and understand.
  - ○ **Hyperparameter Tuning:** Deep learning models have many hyperparameters that need to be tuned.[23]

9.2 Convolutional Neural Networks (CNNs): Image Recognition

Convolutional Neural Networks (CNNs) are a specialized type of neural network designed for processing image data.[24]

- **The Concept of Convolution:**
    - Convolution is a mathematical operation that involves sliding a filter (kernel) over an input image and computing the dot product between the filter and the input.[25]
    - This operation extracts features from the image, such as edges, corners, and textures.[26]
- **CNN Architecture:**
    - **Convolutional Layers:** Apply convolutional filters to extract features from the input image.[27]

- o **Pooling Layers:** Reduce the spatial dimensions of the feature maps, reducing the number of parameters and computational cost.[28]
- o **Activation Functions:** Introduce non-linearity to the network.[29]
- o **Fully Connected Layers:** Connect all neurons in one layer to all neurons in the next layer, used for classification.[30]
- o **Output Layer:** Produces the final classification or regression results.[31]
- **Convolutional Layers in Detail:**
  - o **Filters (Kernels):** Small matrices that are convolved with the input image.
  - o **Feature Maps:** The output of a convolutional layer, representing the extracted features.[32]

- ○ **Stride:** The number of pixels the filter moves across the input image.
- ○ **Padding:** Adding extra pixels around the input image to control the size of the feature maps.
- **Pooling Layers in Detail:**
  - ○ **Max Pooling:** Selects the maximum value in each pooling window.
  - ○ **Average Pooling:** Calculates the average value in each pooling window.
  - ○ **Reduces Spatial Dimensions:** Pooling layers reduce the spatial dimensions of the feature maps, reducing the number of parameters and computational cost.[33]
- **Activation Functions in CNNs:**
  - ○ ReLU is commonly used in convolutional layers.[34]

- Softmax is typically used in the output layer for multiclass classification.[35]
- **Applications of CNNs:**
  - **Image Classification:** Classifying images into different categories.[36]
  - **Object Detection:** Identifying and localizing objects in images.[37]
  - **Image Segmentation:** Dividing an image into meaningful regions.[38]
  - **Face Recognition:** Identifying individuals from their facial images.[39]
  - **Medical Image Analysis:** Assisting in the diagnosis of diseases from medical images.[40]
- **Training CNNs:**
  - CNNs are trained using backpropagation and optimization algorithms, such as Adam.[41]

- Data augmentation techniques, such as rotation and flipping, can be used to increase the size of the training dataset.[42]
- **Pre-trained Models:**
  - Pre-trained CNN models, such as ResNet, VGG, and Inception, are available for transfer learning.[43]
  - Transfer learning involves using a pre-trained model as a starting point for a new task, which can significantly reduce training time and improve performance.[44]

CNNs have revolutionized image recognition by enabling the development of highly accurate and powerful models that can automatically learn relevant features from raw image data.[45]

9.3 Recurrent Neural Networks (RNNs): Sequence Data Analysis

Recurrent Neural Networks (RNNs) are a type of neural network designed to process sequential data, such as text, time series, and audio.[1] They excel at tasks where the order of information is crucial.

- **The Concept of Recurrence:**
  - RNNs have a recurrent connection, which allows them to maintain a "memory" of past inputs.[2]
  - This memory enables them to process sequential data by taking into account the context of previous inputs.[3]
- **RNN Architecture:**
  - RNNs consist of recurrent cells that process the input sequence one element at a time.[4]

- The output of each cell is fed back into the cell as input for the next time step.[5]
- This allows the network to maintain a hidden state that represents the memory of the sequence.
- **Applications of RNNs:**
  - **Natural Language Processing (NLP):**
    - Language modeling: Predicting the next word in a sequence.[6]
    - Machine translation: Translating text from one language to another.[7]
    - Sentiment analysis: Determining the sentiment of a text.[8]
  - **Time Series Analysis:**
    - Stock price prediction: Forecasting future stock prices based on historical data.[9]

- Weather forecasting: Predicting future weather conditions.[10]
- Anomaly detection: Identifying unusual patterns in time series data.[11]
  - **Speech Recognition:** Converting spoken language into text.[12]
  - **Video Analysis:** Analyzing video sequences for tasks such as action recognition.[13]
- **Challenges of RNNs:**
  - **Vanishing Gradient Problem:** The gradients can become very small during backpropagation, making it difficult to train RNNs with long sequences.[14]
  - **Exploding Gradient Problem:** The gradients can become very large during

backpropagation, leading to instability.[15]

- ○ **Difficulty in Capturing Long-Term Dependencies:** RNNs struggle to capture long-range dependencies in sequences.[16]

9.4 Long Short-Term Memory (LSTM) Networks: Handling Long-Term Dependencies

Long Short-Term Memory (LSTM) networks are a specialized type of RNN that addresses the vanishing gradient problem and enables the capture of long-term dependencies.[17]

- **The LSTM Cell:**
  - ○ LSTMs introduce a memory cell that can store information over long periods.[18]

- The LSTM cell uses gating mechanisms to control the flow of information into and out of the cell.[19]
- The gates include:
  - **Forget Gate:** Controls what information to forget from the cell state.
  - **Input Gate:** Controls what new information to add to the cell state.
  - **Output Gate:** Controls what information to output from the cell state.

- **Advantages of LSTMs:**
  - **Mitigate Vanishing Gradient Problem:** LSTMs are less prone to the vanishing gradient problem, allowing them to capture long-term dependencies.[20]
  - **Capture Long-Term Dependencies:** LSTMs can maintain information over long

sequences, making them suitable for tasks with long-range dependencies.[21]

- **Improved Performance:** LSTMs have achieved state-of-the-art results in various sequence modeling tasks.[22]

- **Applications of LSTMs:**
  - LSTMs are widely used in NLP, time series analysis, and other sequence modeling tasks.[23]
  - They are particularly effective in tasks that require capturing long-range dependencies, such as language modeling and machine translation.

- **Gated Recurrent Units (GRUs):**
  - GRUs are a simplified variant of LSTMs that also address the vanishing gradient problem.[24]
  - GRUs have fewer parameters than LSTMs, making them computationally more efficient.[25]

9.5 Practical Implementation: Building Deep Learning Models in Python

Let's demonstrate how to build RNN and LSTM models in Python using Keras/TensorFlow.

- **RNN Example (Text Generation):**

Python

```
import tensorflow as tf
from tensorflow import keras
import numpy as np

# Example data (replace with your text data)
text = "This is an example text for RNN."
chars = sorted(list(set(text)))
char_indices = dict((c, i) for i, c in enumerate(chars))
```

```python
    indices_char = dict((i, c) for i, c in
enumerate(chars))

    # Prepare data
    maxlen = 40
    step = 3
    sentences = []
    next_chars = []
    for i in range(0, len(text) - maxlen, step):
        sentences.append(text[i: i + maxlen])
        next_chars.append(text[i + maxlen])

    x = np.zeros((len(sentences), maxlen,
len(chars)), dtype=np.bool)
    y = np.zeros((len(sentences), len(chars)),
dtype=np.bool)
    for i, sentence in enumerate(sentences):
        for t, char in enumerate(sentence):
            x[i, t, char_indices[char]] = 1
            y[i, char_indices[next_chars[i]]] = 1

    # Build the model
    model = keras.Sequential([
```

```python
    keras.layers.SimpleRNN(128,
input_shape=(maxlen, len(chars))),
    keras.layers.Dense(len(chars),
activation='softmax')
])

    model.compile(optimizer='adam',
loss='categorical_crossentropy')

# Train the model
    model.fit(x,    y,    epochs=20,
batch_size=128)
```

- **LSTM Example (Time Series Prediction):**

Python

```python
import tensorflow as tf
from tensorflow import keras
import numpy as np
```

```
# Example data (replace with your time
series data)
data = np.sin(np.linspace(0, 10, 100))
x_data = []
y_data = []
for i in range(len(data) - 10):
    x_data.append(data[i:i + 10])
    y_data.append(data[i + 10])
x_data = np.array(x_data).reshape(-1, 10, 1)
y_data = np.array(y_data)

# Build the model
model = keras.Sequential([
    keras.layers.LSTM(50, activation='relu', input_shape=(10, 1)),
    keras.layers.Dense(1)
])

model.compile(optimizer='adam', loss='mse')

# Train the model
```

```
model.fit(x_data, y_data, epochs=50,
batch_size=32)
```

By understanding RNNs, LSTMs, and
practical implementation, you'll be
well-equipped to build and train powerful
deep learning models for sequence data
analysis.

CHAPTER 10

Natural Language Processing (NLP): Understanding and Generating Human Language

Natural Language Processing (NLP) is a field of artificial intelligence that focuses on enabling computers to understand, interpret,[1] and generate human language.[23] This chapter will introduce the fundamentals of NLP and explore essential text preprocessing techniques.

10.1 Introduction to NLP: Text Processing and Analysis

NLP bridges the gap between human communication and machine understanding, allowing computers to interact with us in a more natural and intuitive way.[4]

- **The Challenge of Human Language:**
  - Human language is complex, ambiguous, and constantly evolving.[5]
  - It involves various levels of analysis, including phonetics, morphology, syntax, semantics, and pragmatics.[6]
  - NLP aims to develop algorithms and models that can handle this complexity.[7]
- **Key Tasks in NLP:**
  - **Text Classification:** Categorizing text into predefined classes (e.g., sentiment analysis, spam detection).[8]
  - **Named Entity Recognition (NER):** Identifying and classifying named entities in text (e.g., people, organizations, locations).[9]
  - **Part-of-Speech (POS) Tagging:** Assigning

grammatical tags to words in a sentence (e.g., noun, verb, adjective).[10]

- ○ **Sentiment Analysis:** Determining the emotional tone or sentiment of a text.[11]
- ○ **Machine Translation:** Translating text from one language to another.[12]
- ○ **Question Answering:** Answering questions based on a given text or knowledge base.[13]
- ○ **Text Summarization:** Generating concise summaries of longer texts.[14]
- ○ **Text Generation:** Generating human-like text, such as stories or articles.[15]
- ○ **Information Retrieval:** Finding relevant information in a large collection of documents.[16]
- • **Applications of NLP:**

- **Virtual Assistants:** Enabling voice-based interaction with devices and services.[17]
- **Chatbots:** Providing automated customer support and conversational interfaces.[18]
- **Search Engines:** Improving the relevance and accuracy of search results.[19]
- **Social Media Analysis:** Understanding public opinion and trends on social media platforms.
- **Medical Diagnosis:** Analyzing medical records and research papers to assist in diagnosis.[20]
- **Legal Document Analysis:** Extracting key information from legal documents.[21]
- **Content Generation:** Generating news articles, product descriptions, and other types of content.[22]
- **The NLP Pipeline:**

- NLP tasks often involve a pipeline of steps, including:
  - **Text Preprocessing:** Cleaning and preparing the text for analysis.[23]
  - **Feature Extraction:** Converting text into numerical representations that machine learning models can understand.[24]
  - **Model Training:** Training a machine learning model on the preprocessed and featurized data.
  - **Model Evaluation:** Evaluating the performance of the model on a testing dataset.[25]

10.2 Text Preprocessing: Tokenization, Stemming, and Lemmatization

Text preprocessing is a crucial step in NLP that involves cleaning and preparing text data for analysis.[26]

- **Tokenization:**
    - Tokenization is the process of splitting a text into individual words or tokens.[27]
    - Tokens are the basic units of text that are processed by NLP algorithms.[28]
    - Tokenization can be performed using various methods, such as whitespace tokenization or regular expressions.[29]
    - Example:
        - Input: "The quick brown fox jumps over the lazy dog."

- Output: ["The", "quick", "brown", "fox", "jumps", "over", "the", "lazy", "dog", "."]
- **Cleaning:**
  - Cleaning involves removing irrelevant characters, such as punctuation, special characters, and HTML tags.
  - It also involves converting text to lowercase to ensure consistency.
- **Stop Word Removal:**
  - Stop words are common words that are often removed from text because they do not carry significant meaning (e.g., "the," "a," "is").[30]
  - Removing stop words can reduce the dimensionality of the data and improve the performance of NLP models.[31]
- **Stemming:**

- Stemming is the process of reducing words to their root form by removing suffixes.[32]
- Stemming algorithms are typically rule-based and can sometimes produce incorrect stems.[33]
- Example:
    - Input: "running," "runs," "ran"
    - Output: "run"

- **Lemmatization:**
    - Lemmatization is similar to stimming, but it reduces words to their base or dictionary form (lemma).[34]
    - Lemmatization uses a vocabulary and morphological analysis to find the correct lemma.[35]
    - Lemmatization is generally more accurate than stemming, but it is also more computationally expensive.[36]

- Example:
  - Input: "better," "best"
  - Output: "good"
- **N-grams:**
  - N-grams are sequences of N consecutive words or tokens.[37]
  - N-grams can capture the context of words and improve the performance of NLP models.[38]
  - Example:
    - Input: "The quick brown fox"
    - Bi-grams: ["The quick", "quick brown", "brown fox"][39]
- **Text Normalization:**
  - Text normalization involves converting text to a standard format, such as Unicode.[40]
  - This ensures that text from different sources can be processed consistently.
- **Libraries for Text Preprocessing:**

- **NLTK (Natural Language Toolkit):** A comprehensive library for NLP tasks, including tokenization, stemming, lemmatization, and stop word removal.[41]
- **spaCy:** A fast and efficient library for NLP tasks, with support for tokenization, POS tagging, NER, and more.[42]
- **Scikit-learn:** A machine learning library with tools for text preprocessing, such as CountVectorizer and TfidfVectorizer.[43]
- **Transformers (Hugging Face):** A library that provides state-of-the-art pretrained models and tokenizers.

By mastering text preprocessing techniques, you'll be well-equipped to prepare text data for a wide range of NLP tasks.

10.3 Word Embeddings: Representing Words as Vectors

Word embeddings are a crucial advancement in NLP that allows us to represent words as dense, low-dimensional vectors, capturing semantic relationships between words.[1]

- **The Limitations of Traditional Representations:**
    - Traditional representations, such as one-hot encoding, represent words as sparse, high-dimensional vectors.
    - These representations do not capture semantic relationships between words.
    - For example, "king" and "queen" are treated as completely unrelated words.
- **The Concept of Word Embeddings:**

- Word embeddings represent words as dense, low-dimensional vectors in a continuous vector space.[2]
- Similar words are located close to each other in the vector space.[3]
- Word embeddings capture semantic relationships between words, such as analogy and similarity.[4]

- **Word2Vec:**
  - Word2Vec is a popular algorithm for learning word embeddings.[5]
  - It uses a shallow neural network to predict the context of a word or the word given its context.[6]
  - **Continuous Bag of Words (CBOW):** Predicts a target word given its surrounding context words.[7]

- o **Skip-gram:** Predicts the surrounding context words given a target word.[8]
- o Word2Vec embeddings are trained on large text corpora.[9]
- **GloVe (Global Vectors for Word Representation):**
  - o GloVe is another popular algorithm for learning word embeddings.[10]
  - o It leverages global word-word co-occurrence statistics to learn word vectors.[11]
  - o GloVe embeddings are also trained on large text corpora.[12]
- **FastText:**
  - o FastText is an extension of Word2Vec that represents words as n-grams of characters.[13]
  - o This allows FastText to learn embeddings for out-of-vocabulary words.

- ○ FastText is particularly useful for morphologically rich languages.[14]
- **Advantages of Word Embeddings:**
  - ○ **Capture Semantic Relationships:** Word embeddings capture semantic relationships between words, improving the performance of NLP models.[15]
  - ○ **Reduce Dimensionality:** Word embeddings reduce the dimensionality of text data, making it more efficient to process.[16]
  - ○ **Improve Generalization:** Word embeddings can improve the generalization ability of NLP models.[17]
- **Applications of Word Embeddings:**

- ○ **Text Classification:** Improving the accuracy of text classification models.
- ○ **Sentiment Analysis:** Capturing the nuances of sentiment in text.
- ○ **Machine Translation:** Improving the quality of machine translation.
- ○ **Question Answering:** Understanding the semantic relationships between words in questions and answers.
- ○ **Information Retrieval:** Improving the relevance of search results.
- **Pre-trained Word Embeddings:**
  - ○ Pre-trained word embeddings, such as Word2Vec, GloVe, and FastText, are available for use in NLP tasks.[18]
  - ○ These embeddings are trained on large text corpora and can be

used as a starting point for new tasks.[19]

10.4   Sentiment   Analysis: Understanding Emotions in Text

Sentiment analysis is a crucial NLP task that aims to determine the emotional tone or sentiment of a text.[20]

- **The   Concept   of   Sentiment Analysis:**
    - Sentiment   analysis   involves classifying   text   as   positive, negative, or neutral.[21]
    - It can also involve identifying more granular emotions, such as joy, sadness, anger, and fear.
- **Applications   of   Sentiment Analysis:**
    - **Social   Media   Monitoring:** Understanding   public   opinion

and trends on social media platforms.

- **Customer Feedback Analysis:** Analyzing customer reviews and feedback to identify areas for improvement.
- **Product Reviews Analysis:** Determining the overall sentiment of product reviews.
- **Brand Monitoring:** Tracking the sentiment associated with a brand.
- **Political Analysis:** Analyzing the sentiment of political discourse.

- **Approaches to Sentiment Analysis:**
  - **Lexicon-Based Approach:** Using a lexicon of words and their associated sentiment scores to determine the sentiment of a text.
  - **Machine Learning Approach:** Training a machine

learning model on labeled data to classify the sentiment of a text.

- ○ **Deep Learning Approach:** Using deep learning models, such as RNNs and CNNs, to capture the nuances of sentiment in text.[22]

- **Challenges of Sentiment Analysis:**
  - ○ **Sarcasm and Irony:** Detecting sarcasm and irony can be challenging for sentiment analysis models.
  - ○ **Context Dependence:** The sentiment of a word or phrase can depend on its context.
  - ○ **Subjectivity:** Sentiment is subjective and can vary depending on the individual.
  - ○ **Language Variations:** Sentiment analysis models need to handle different languages and dialects.[23]

- **Evaluation Metrics for Sentiment Analysis:**
  - Accuracy, precision, recall, F1-score, confusion matrix.

10.5 Practical Implementation: Building NLP Applications in Python

Let's demonstrate how to build NLP applications in Python using libraries like NLTK, spaCy, and Scikit-learn.

- **Sentiment Analysis Example (Using TextBlob):**

Python

```
from textblob import TextBlob

text = "This is a great movie!"
```

```python
blob = TextBlob(text)
sentiment = blob.sentiment.polarity

if sentiment > 0:
    print("Positive sentiment")
elif sentiment < 0:
    print("Negative sentiment")
else:
    print("Neutral sentiment")
```

- **Word Embeddings Example (Using Gensim):**

Python

```python
from gensim.models import Word2Vec

sentences = [["This", "is", "a", "sentence"],
["This", "is", "another", "sentence"]]
model = Word2Vec(sentences,
min_count=1)
vector = model.wv["sentence"]
```

```
similar_words =
model.wv.most_similar("sentence")
```

- **Text Classification Example (Using Scikit-learn):**

Python

```
from sklearn.feature_extraction.text
import TfidfVectorizer
from sklearn.naive_bayes import
MultinomialNB
from sklearn.pipeline import Pipeline
from sklearn.model_selection import
train_test_split
from sklearn.metrics import
accuracy_score

# Example data
X = ["This is positive", "This is negative",
"Another positive", "Another negative"]
y = [1, 0, 1, 0]
```

```python
    X_train, X_test, y_train, y_test =
train_test_split(X, y, test_size=0.2)

   model = Pipeline([
     ('tfidf', TfidfVectorizer()),
     ('clf', MultinomialNB())
   ])

   model.fit(X_train, y_train)
   y_pred = model.predict(X_test)

    accuracy = accuracy_score(y_test,
y_pred)
   print(f"Accuracy: {accuracy}")
```

By understanding word embeddings, sentiment analysis, and practical implementation, you'll be well-equipped to build a wide range of NLP applications.

CHAPTER 11

Reinforcement Learning: Learning Through Interaction with an Environment

Reinforcement Learning (RL) is a paradigm of machine learning where an agent learns to make decisions by interacting with an environment.[1] This chapter will introduce the fundamentals of RL, explore Q-learning and Deep RL, and provide practical implementation examples.

11.1 Introduction to Reinforcement Learning: Agents and Environments

RL is inspired by how humans and animals learn through trial and error, receiving feedback in the form of rewards or punishments.[2]

- **The RL Framework:**
  - **Agent:** The decision-making entity that interacts with the environment.[3]
  - **Environment:** The external world with which the agent interacts.
  - **State (s):** A representation of the environment at a particular time.[4]
  - **Action (a):** A decision made by the agent in a given state.
  - **Reward (r):** A feedback signal from the environment indicating the desirability of an action.[5]
  - **Policy (π):** A mapping from states to actions, defining the agent's behavior.[6]
- **The Goal of RL:**
  - The goal of RL is to learn an optimal policy that maximizes the cumulative reward over time.[7]

- The agent learns through trial and error, exploring the environment and exploiting its knowledge to make better decisions.[8]
- **Key Concepts:**
  - **Markov Decision Process (MDP):** A mathematical framework for modeling sequential decision-making problems.[9]
  - **Discount Factor (γ):** A parameter that determines the importance of future rewards.[10]
  - **Value Function (V):** A function that estimates the expected cumulative reward from a given state.[11]
  - **Q-function (Q):** A function that estimates the expected cumulative reward from taking a given action in a given state.
- **Types of RL:**

- **Model-Based RL:** The agent learns a model of the environment and uses it to plan its actions.[12]
- **Model-Free RL:** The agent learns directly from experience without learning a model of the environment.[13]
- **On-Policy RL:** The agent learns the policy it is currently following.
- **Off-Policy RL:** The agent learns a policy that is different from the one it is currently following.

- **Applications of RL:**
  - **Game Playing:** Training AI agents to play games at a superhuman level.
  - **Robotics:** Controlling robots to perform complex tasks.[14]
  - **Autonomous Driving:** Enabling vehicles to navigate

and make decisions in real-world environments.

- ○ **Resource Management:** Optimizing the allocation of resources in various domains.[15]
- ○ **Recommendation Systems:** Providing personalized recommendations to users.[16]
- ○ **Finance:** Optimizing trading strategies and portfolio management.[17]

11.2 Q-Learning: Learning Optimal Policies

Q-learning is a popular model-free, off-policy RL algorithm that learns an optimal policy by estimating the Q-function.[18]

- **The Q-Function:**

- The Q-function, Q(s, a), estimates the expected cumulative reward from taking action 'a' in state 's'.
- Q-learning aims to learn the optimal Q-function, Q*(s, a), which maximizes the expected cumulative reward.[19]

- **The Q-Learning Algorithm:**
  - **Initialization:** Initialize the Q-function with arbitrary values.
  - **Exploration vs. Exploitation:** Choose an action 'a' in state 's' using an exploration-exploitation strategy (e.g., ε-greedy).[20]
  - **Take Action:** Take action 'a' and observe the next state 's'' and reward 'r'.
  - **Update Q-function:** Update the Q-function using the Q-learning update rule:
    - $Q(s, a) = Q(s, a) + \alpha * (r + \gamma * \max(Q(s', a')) - Q(s, a))$

- Where:
    - α is the learning rate.
    - γ is the discount factor.[21]
    - max(Q(s', a')) is the maximum Q-value for the next state 's".
  - **Iteration:** Repeat steps 2-4 until convergence.[22]
- **ε-greedy Strategy:**
  - The ε-greedy strategy balances exploration and exploitation.[23]
  - With probability ε, the agent chooses a random action (exploration).
  - With probability 1-ε, the agent chooses the action with the highest Q-value (exploitation).
- **Advantages of Q-Learning:**
  - Simple and easy to implement.
  - Model-free, meaning it does not require a model of the environment.[24]

- Off-policy, meaning it can learn from experiences generated by any policy.
- **Disadvantages of Q-Learning:**
  - Can be slow to converge for large state spaces.
  - Requires storing the Q-function in a table, which can be memory-intensive.[25]

11.3 Deep Reinforcement Learning: Combining Deep Learning and Reinforcement Learning

Deep Reinforcement Learning (Deep RL) combines the power of deep learning with the decision-making capabilities of RL.[26]

- **The Need for Deep RL:**

- Traditional RL algorithms, such as Q-learning, can struggle with large state spaces.[27]
- Deep learning models can learn complex representations of high-dimensional state spaces.
- Deep RL leverages deep neural networks to approximate the Q-function or policy.[28]

- **Deep Q-Network (DQN):**
  - DQN is a popular Deep RL algorithm that uses a deep neural network to approximate the Q-function.[29]
  - DQN addresses the challenges of Q-learning in high-dimensional state spaces.[30]
  - DQN uses experience replay and target networks to stabilize training.[31]

- **Policy Gradient Methods:**
  - Policy gradient methods directly learn the policy by optimizing a policy objective function.[32]

- These methods are suitable for continuous action spaces.
- REINFORCE and Actor-Critic are examples of policy gradient methods.[33]
- **Advantages of Deep RL:**
  - Can handle high-dimensional state spaces.[34]
  - Can learn complex policies.
  - Has achieved state-of-the-art results in various domains.[35]
- **Disadvantages of Deep RL:**
  - Can be computationally expensive.
  - Requires careful tuning of hyperparameters.
  - Can be unstable and difficult to train.

11.4 Practical Implementation: Building Reinforcement Learning Agents in Python

Implementing RL agents in Python involves using libraries that provide environments, algorithms, and tools for training and evaluating agents.[1] We'll focus on using OpenAI Gym for environments and TensorFlow/PyTorch for implementing RL algorithms.

1. Using OpenAI Gym for Environments

OpenAI Gym is a toolkit for developing and comparing RL algorithms.[2] It provides a wide range of environments, from classic control problems to Atari games.[3]

- **Installation:**
- Bash

```
pip install gym
```

-
-
- **Creating an Environment:**
- Python

```
import gym
```

```
env = gym.make('CartPole-v1')  # Create the
CartPole environment
```

-
  - CartPole-v1 is a classic control problem where the goal is to balance a pole on a cart.
  - Gym provides various environments, such as MountainCar-v0, Acrobot-v1, and Atari games.

- **Environment Interaction:**
- Python

```
state = env.reset()  # Reset the environment and get the initial state

action = env.action_space.sample()  # Sample a random action

new_state, reward, done, info = env.step(action)  # Take the action and get the results
```

-
  - env.reset() returns the initial state of the environment.
  - env.action_space.sample() samples a random action from the action space.
  - env.step(action) takes an action and returns the new state, reward, done flag, and info.

- done is a boolean flag that indicates whether the episode has terminated.
- **Observation and Action Spaces:**
- Python

```
print(env.observation_space)   # Print the observation space

print(env.action_space)  # Print the action space
```

-
  - env.observation_space describes the structure of the state.
  - env.action_space describes the structure of the action.

2. Implementing Q-Learning

Q-learning is a model-free, off-policy RL algorithm that learns an optimal policy by estimating the Q-function.[4]

- **Q-Learning Implementation:**
  - Python

```python
import gym

import numpy as np


env = gym.make('FrozenLake-v1')

Q = np.zeros([env.observation_space.n,
env.action_space.n])  # Initialize Q-table

alpha = 0.8  # Learning rate

gamma = 0.95  # Discount factor

episodes = 2000  # Number of episodes
```

```python
for i in range(episodes):

    state = env.reset()

    done = False

    while not done:

        action = np.argmax(Q[state, :] +
np.random.randn(1, env.action_space.n) *
(1. / (i + 1)))   # Epsilon-greedy action
selection

        new_state, reward, done, _ =
env.step(action)

        Q[state, action] = Q[state, action] +
alpha * (reward + gamma *
np.max(Q[new_state, :]) - Q[state, action])
# Q-learning update

        state = new_state


print("Q-table:")

print(Q)
```

-

  - We initialize a Q-table with zeros.[5]
  - We use an epsilon-greedy strategy to balance exploration and exploitation.
  - We update the Q-table using the Q-learning update rule.

3. Implementing Deep Q-Networks (DQN)

DQN uses a deep neural network to approximate the Q-function, enabling it to handle high-dimensional state spaces.[6]

- **DQN Implementation (TensorFlow):**
- Python

```
import gym
```

```python
import tensorflow as tf

from collections import deque

import random

import numpy as np


env = gym.make('CartPole-v1')

state_size                          =
env.observation_space.shape[0]

action_size = env.action_space.n


model = tf.keras.Sequential([

    tf.keras.layers.Dense(24, activation='relu',
input_dim=state_size),

                tf.keras.layers.Dense(24,
activation='relu'),
```

```python
        tf.keras.layers.Dense(action_size,
activation='linear')

])

model.compile(loss='mse',
optimizer=tf.keras.optimizers.Adam(lr=0.0
01))


memory  =  deque(maxlen=2000)      #
Experience replay buffer

gamma = 0.95  # Discount factor

epsilon = 1.0  # Exploration rate

epsilon_decay = 0.995

epsilon_min = 0.01


for episode in range(500):
    state = env.reset()
```

```python
    state = np.reshape(state, [1, state_size])

    done = False

    while not done:

        if np.random.rand() <= epsilon:

            action = random.randrange(action_size)

        else:

            action = np.argmax(model.predict(state)[0])

        new_state, reward, done, _ = env.step(action)

        reward = reward if not done else -10  # Penalize for failure

        new_state = np.reshape(new_state, [1, state_size])

        memory.append((state, action, reward, new_state, done))
```

```python
        state = new_state

        if len(memory) > 32:

                        minibatch  =
random.sample(memory, 32)

            for state, action, reward, new_state,
done in minibatch:

                target = reward

                if not done:

                        target = reward + gamma *
np.amax(model.predict(new_state)[0])

                target_f = model.predict(state)

                target_f[0][action] = target

                model.fit(state, target_f, epochs=1,
verbose=0)

        if epsilon > epsilon_min:

            epsilon *= epsilon_decay
```

-
  - We build a deep neural network to approximate the Q-function.[7]
  - We use experience replay to stabilize training.[8]
  - We use an epsilon-greedy strategy for exploration.

Key Considerations:

- **Hyperparameter Tuning:** RL algorithms have many hyperparameters that need to be tuned for optimal performance.[9]
- **Exploration vs. Exploitation:** Balancing exploration and exploitation is crucial for learning effective policies.[10]
- **Experience Replay:** Experience replay is a technique that stores past experiences and samples them randomly to update the Q-function.[11]

- **Target Networks:** Target networks are used to stabilize training by providing a stable target for the Q-function update.[12]
- **Evaluation:** Evaluating the performance of RL agents involves measuring their cumulative reward and other metrics.[13]

By understanding these practical implementation details, you can begin building and training your own RL agents in Python.

Part IV

Practical Applications and Future Directions

CHAPTER 12

Building AI Applications: Real-World Projects

This chapter will guide you through four practical AI projects, demonstrating how to apply the concepts and techniques learned in previous chapters. We'll also discuss best practices for building robust and effective AI applications.

12.1 Project 1: Image Classification with CNNs

- **Objective:** Build a CNN model to classify images from a dataset (e.g., CIFAR-10, MNIST).[1]
- **Dataset:**
    1. CIFAR-10: 60,000 32x32 color images in 10 classes.[2]

2. MNIST: 70,000 grayscale images of handwritten digits.

- **Implementation Steps:**
    1. **Data Loading and Preprocessing:**
        - Load the dataset using Keras or TensorFlow datasets.[3]
        - Normalize pixel values to the range [0, 1].
        - One-hot encodes the labels.
        - Split the data into training and testing sets.
    2. **CNN Model Architecture:**
        - Build a sequential CNN model using Keras.
        - Include convolutional layers, pooling layers, and fully connected layers.
        - Use ReLU activation functions in convolutional and fully connected layers.

- Use a softmax activation function in the output layer.

3. **Model Compilation and Training:**
    - Compile the model with an optimizer (e.g., Adam), loss function (e.g., categorical cross entropy), and metrics (e.g., accuracy).
    - Train the model using the fit() method.
    - Monitor the training process using validation data.

4. **Model Evaluation:**
    - Evaluate the model's performance on the testing set using the evaluate() method.
    - Visualize the confusion matrix and classification report.

- Analyze the model's performance and identify areas for improvement.
- **Key Libraries:** TensorFlow/Keras, Matplotlib, Scikit-learn.

12.2 Project 2: Sentiment Analysis of Social Media Data

- **Objective:** Build a sentiment analysis model to classify the sentiment of social media posts (e.g., tweets).
- **Dataset:**
    1. Twitter Sentiment Analysis Dataset.
    2. IMDB Movie Reviews Dataset.
- **Implementation Steps:**
    1. **Data Collection and Preprocessing:**
        - Collect social media data using APIs (e.g., Twitter API).[4]

- Clean the text data by removing URLs, punctuation, and special characters.
- Tokenize the text data.
- Remove stop words.
- Apply stemming or lemmatization.

2. **Feature Extraction:**
   - Use TF-IDF vectorization to convert text data into numerical features.
   - Alternatively, use pre-trained word embeddings (e.g., Word2Vec, GloVe).

3. **Model Training:**
   - Train a classification model (e.g., Naive Bayes, Logistic Regression, RNN, LSTM) on the featurized data.

- Use cross-validation to evaluate the model's performance.
4. **Model Evaluation:**
    - Evaluate the model's performance using metrics like accuracy, precision, recall, and F1-score.
    - Analyze the model's performance and identify areas for improvement.
- **Key Libraries:** NLTK, Scikit-learn, TextBlob, Transformers (Hugging Face).

12.3 Project 3: Building a Simple Chatbot

- **Objective:** Build a chatbot that can respond to user queries based on a predefined knowledge base.
- **Implementation Steps:**
    1. **Knowledge Base Creation:**

- Create a knowledge base of question-answer pairs.
- Store the knowledge base in a JSON or CSV file.

2. **Text Preprocessing:**
   - Preprocess the user input and knowledge base text using tokenization, stop word removal, and stemming/lemmatization.

3. **Intent Recognition:**
   - Use a simple rule-based or machine learning approach to identify the user's intent.
   - Alternatively, use pre trained transformer models for intent detection.

4. **Response Generation:**
   - Retrieve the appropriate response from the knowledge base based on the identified intent.

- Use a simple template-based or generative approach to generate a response.
5. **Chatbot Interface:**
  - Create a simple command-line or web-based interface for the chatbot.
- **Key Libraries:** NLTK, Scikit-learn, Transformers (Hugging Face).

12.4 Project 4: Predictive Maintenance with Regression.

- **Objective:** Develop a regression model that predicts the remaining useful life (RUL) of machinery based on sensor data.
- **Dataset:**
  1. NASA C-MAPSS dataset.
- **Implementation Steps:**

1. **Data Loading and Preprocessing:**
   - Load the sensor data from CSV files.
   - Clean and preprocess the data by handling missing values and outliers.
   - Feature engineering: create rolling averages, moving variances, etc.
   - Create a target variable representing the RUL.
   - Split the data into training and testing sets.
2. **Regression Model Training:**
   - Train a regression model (e.g., Linear Regression, Polynomial Regression, Random Forest Regression, LSTM) on the preprocessed data.
   - Use cross-validation to evaluate the model's performance.

3. **Model Evaluation:**
   - Evaluate the model's performance using metrics like MSE, RMSE, and R-squared.
   - Visualize the predicted RUL vs. actual RUL.
   - Analyze the model's errors.
- **Key Libraries:** Pandas, Scikit-learn, TensorFlow/Keras, Matplotlib.

12.5 Best Practices for Building AI Projects

- **Define Clear Objectives:** Clearly define the problem you are trying to solve and the goals of your AI project.
- **Data Collection and Preparation:** Collect high-quality data and preprocess it carefully.
- **Experimentation and Iteration:** Experiment with different algorithms

and techniques, and iterate on your model based on the results.

- **Model Evaluation:** Evaluate your model's performance using appropriate metrics and techniques.
- **Documentation:** Document your code, data, and model to ensure reproducibility and maintainability.[5]
- **Version Control:** Use version control (e.g., Git) to track changes to your code and data.[6]
- **Ethical Considerations:** Consider the ethical implications of your AI project and ensure that it is used responsibly.
- **Deployment:** Plan for the deployment of your AI model and consider the scalability and maintainability of your application.
- **Monitoring:** Monitor the performance of your deployed AI model and make adjustments as needed.

- **Collaboration:** Collaborate with other team members and stakeholders to ensure the success of your AI project.
- **Continuous Learning:** Stay up-to-date with the latest advancements in AI and machine learning.
- **Start Small:** Begin with smaller, manageable projects to gain experience and build confidence.
- **Understand your Data:** Thoroughly understand the data you are working with, including its sources, characteristics, and potential biases.
- **Use appropriate tools:** Select the right tools and libraries for your project, based on the specific requirements and constraints.
- **Test Thoroughly:** Test your model thoroughly to ensure that it meets the desired performance criteria.

- **Seek Feedback:** Seek feedback from other AI practitioners and domain experts to improve your project.

By following these best practices, you can build robust and effective AI applications that solve real-world problems.

CHAPTER 13

Deploying AI Models: From Development to Production

Deploying AI models is the crucial step that bridges the gap between development and real-world application.[1] This chapter will guide you through the process of deploying AI models, ensuring they are accessible, scalable, and maintainable.

13.1 Model Serialization and Persistence

Before deploying a model, it needs to be serialized and persisted, which involves saving the trained model's parameters and structure to a file.[2]

- **Purpose of Serialization:**

- o **Storage:** Saving the trained model for later use without retraining.
- o **Transfer:** Sharing the model across different environments or platforms.
- o **Deployment:** Loading the model into a production environment.[3]
- **Techniques for Serialization:**
  - o **Pickle (Python):** A built-in Python module for serializing and deserializing Python objects.[4] Suitable for simple models.
  - o Python

```python
import pickle

# Save the model
with open('model.pkl', 'wb') as f:
    pickle.dump(model, f)
```

```
# Load the model
with open('model.pkl', 'rb') as f:
    loaded_model = pickle.load(f)
```

- ○
- ○
- ○ **Joblib (Python):** An optimized library for serializing NumPy arrays and large objects, often preferred over Pickle for machine learning models.[5]
- ○ Python

```
import joblib

# Save the model
joblib.dump(model, 'model.joblib')

# Load the model
```

loaded_model = joblib.load('model.joblib')

- ○
- ○
- ○ **TensorFlow SavedModel:** TensorFlow's recommended format for saving and loading models, including weights, architecture, and variables.[6]

import tensorflow as tf

```
# Save the model
tf.saved_model.save(model, 'saved_model')

# Load the model
loaded_model = tf.saved_model.load('saved_model')
```
```
```

* **ONNX (Open Neural Network Exchange):** An open format for representing machine learning models, enabling interoperability between different frameworks.

```python
import onnx
import tf2onnx

# Convert TensorFlow model to ONNX
onnx_model, _ = tf2onnx.convert.from_keras(model)
onnx.save(onnx_model, 'model.onnx')
```

- **Best Practices:**
  - Choose the serialization method based on the framework and model complexity.
  - Ensure that the environment used for loading the model has the same dependencies as the training environment.

○ Consider using version control for serialized models.

13.2 Web Deployment with Flask/FastAPI

Web deployment allows you to make your AI model accessible through a web interface, enabling users to interact with it remotely.[7]

- **Flask (Python):** A lightweight web framework for building simple web applications.[8]
  - ○ **Installation:**
  - ○ Bash

```
pip install Flask
```

-
-
- **Example:**
- Python

```python
from flask import Flask, request, jsonify
import joblib

app = Flask(__name__)
model = joblib.load('model.joblib')

@app.route('/predict', methods=['POST'])
def predict():
    data = request.get_json()
    prediction = model.predict([data['features']])
    return jsonify({'prediction': prediction.tolist()})

if __name__ == '__main__':
    app.run(debug=True)
```

- ○
- ○
-
- **FastAPI (Python):** A modern, fast (high-performance) web framework for building APIs.[9]
  - ○ **Installation:**
  - ○ Bash

pip install fastapi uvicorn

- ○
- ○
- ○ **Example:**
- ○ Python

from fastapi import FastAPI
import joblib

```python
from pedantic import BaseModel

app = FastAPI()
model = joblib.load('model.joblib')

class InputData(BaseModel):
    features: list

@app.post('/predict')
def predict(data: InputData):
                        prediction    =
model.predict([data.features])
    return {'prediction': prediction.tolist()}

if __name__ == '__main__':
    import uvicorn
        uvicorn.run(app,   host="127.0.0.1",
port=8000)
```

- o
- o

-

- **Best Practices:**

o Use a virtual environment to manage dependencies.
o Implement input validation and error handling.
o Secure your API using authentication and authorization.
o Use a production-ready WSGI server (e.g., Gunicorn, uWSGI).

13.3 Cloud Deployment: AWS, Google Cloud, and Azure

Cloud platforms provide scalable and reliable infrastructure for deploying AI models.[10]

- **AWS (Amazon Web Services):**
  o **SageMaker:** A fully managed machine learning service for building, training, and deploying models.[11]

- ○ **Lambda:** A serverless compute service for running code without managing servers.[12]
- ○ **EC2:** Elastic Compute Cloud for deploying models on virtual servers.[13]
- **Google Cloud Platform (GCP):**
  - ○ **Vertex AI:** A unified machine learning platform for building, training, and deploying models.[14]
  - ○ **Cloud Functions:** A serverless compute service for running code in response to events.[15]
  - ○ **Compute Engine:** Virtual machines for deploying models.[16]
- **Azure (Microsoft Azure):**
  - ○ **Azure Machine Learning:** A cloud-based machine learning service for building, training, and deploying models.

- ○ **Azure Functions:** A serverless compute service for running code on demand.[17]
- ○ **Azure Virtual Machines:** Virtual machines for deploying models.[18]
- **Best Practices:**
  - ○ Choose the cloud platform that best suits your needs and budget.
  - ○ Use managed services to simplify deployment and maintenance.
  - ○ Implement auto-scaling to handle varying traffic.
  - ○ Monitor the performance and cost of your deployed models.

13.4 Containerization with Docker

Docker allows you to package your AI model and its dependencies into a container, ensuring consistency and portability across different environments.[19]

- **Docker Basics:**
    - **Image:** A read-only template with instructions for creating a container.
    - **Container:** A running instance of an image.
    - **Dockerfile:** A text file that contains instructions for building a Docker image.[20]
- **Example Dockerfile:**
- Dockerfile

```
FROM python:3.9-slim
```

WORKDIR /app

COPY requirements.txt .
RUN pip install --no-cache-dir -r requirements.txt

COPY . .

CMD ["uvicorn", "main:app", "--host", "0.0.0.0", "--port", "8000"]

-
-
- **Building and Running a Docker Container:**
- Bash

```bash
docker build -t my-ai-app .
docker run -p 8000:8000 my-ai-app
```

-
-

- **Best Practices:**
  - Use a minimal base image to reduce the size of the container.
  - Install only the necessary dependencies.
  - Use multi-stage builds to optimize the image size.
  - Use environment variables for configuration.

13.5 Monitoring and Maintaining Deployed Models

Monitoring and maintaining deployed models is crucial for ensuring their reliability and performance over time.[21]

- **Monitoring Metrics:**
  - **Latency:** The time it takes for the model to respond to a request.

- Throughput: The number of requests the model can handle per second.
- Accuracy: The performance of the model on new data.
- Data Drift: Changes in the distribution of input data.[22]
- Model Drift: Changes in the performance of the model over time.[23]

- **Monitoring Tools:**
  - CloudWatch (AWS): A monitoring and logging service for AWS resources.
  - Stackdriver (GCP): A monitoring, logging, and diagnostics service for GCP.
  - Azure Monitor (Azure): A monitoring service for Azure resources.
  - Prometheus and Grafana: Open-source monitoring and visualization tools.[24]
- **Maintenance Tasks:**

- **Model Retraining:** Retraining the model with new data to maintain its accuracy.
- **Model Updating:** Updating the model with new features or algorithms.
- **Security Updates:** Applying security patches to the deployed environment.
- **Scaling:** Adjusting the resources allocated to the model to handle varying traffic.

- **Best Practices:**
  - Implement automated monitoring and alerting.
  - Use version control for deployed models and configurations.
  - Establish a process for model retraining and updating.
  - Regularly review and update the monitoring and maintenance plan.

By following these guidelines, you can successfully deploy and maintain AI models in production environments.

CHAPTER 14

The Future of AI: Emerging Trends and Technologies

The landscape of AI is in a state of perpetual transformation, driven by relentless innovation and a thirst for solutions to complex problems.[1] This chapter aims to provide a comprehensive exploration of the pivotal trends shaping the future of AI.

14.1 Explainable AI (XAI): Making AI Transparent

The increasing complexity of AI models, especially deep learning networks, has led to a "black box" problem, where understanding the reasoning behind a model's decisions becomes challenging.[2] This lack of transparency can hinder trust, accountability, and ethical deployment.[3] Explainable AI (XAI) emerges as a crucial discipline to address this challenge.[4]

- **The Urgent Need for Transparency:**
  - **Building Trust:** In domains like healthcare and finance, where decisions have significant consequences, trust is paramount.[5] XAI provides the necessary transparency to build confidence in AI systems.[6]
  - **Regulatory Compliance:** As AI becomes more integrated into regulated industries, compliance with transparency requirements becomes mandatory.[7]
  - **Ethical AI:** Ensuring fairness and mitigating biases requires understanding how models arrive at their conclusions.[8]
  - **Debugging and Improvement:** Identifying the

root causes of errors in AI models becomes possible with XAI, leading to better model performance.[9]

- **Human-AI Collaboration:** XAI enables humans to understand and collaborate effectively with AI systems.

- **Key XAI Techniques:**
  - **Feature Importance:** Techniques like permutation importance and SHAP values help identify which features contribute most to a model's predictions.[10]
  - **LIME (Local Interpretable Model-agnostic Explanations):** LIME approximates complex models with simpler, interpretable models locally, providing insights into individual predictions.[11]

- **SHAP (SHapley Additive exPlanations):** Based on game theory, SHAP values quantify the contribution of each feature to a prediction, ensuring fairness and consistency.[12]
- **Rule Extraction:** Extracting human-readable rules from complex models, making them more understandable.[13]
- **Attention Mechanisms:** Visualizing which parts of the input a model focuses on, especially in NLP and image recognition tasks.[14]
- **Counterfactual Explanations:** Providing alternative scenarios to understand how changes in input features would affect predictions.[15]

- **Challenges and Future Directions:**

- Scalability: Developing XAI techniques that can handle large datasets and complex models efficiently.[16]
- Standardization: Establishing standardized metrics and evaluation methods for XAI.
- Domain Adaptation: Tailoring XAI techniques to specific domains and applications.[17]
- Real-time Explanations: Developing XAI methods that can provide explanations in real-time for dynamic applications.
- User-centric XAI: Designing XAI tools that are accessible and understandable to non-experts.

14.2 Generative AI: Creating New Content

Generative AI is a burgeoning field that focuses on developing models capable of creating novel content, from images and text to music and code.[18] This technology is poised to revolutionize creative industries and beyond.

- **The Transformative Potential of Generative AI:**
  - **Creative Content Generation:** Generating high-quality images, videos, and music for entertainment, advertising, and design.[19]
  - **Data Augmentation:** Creating synthetic data to train AI models, especially when real-world data is scarce.[20]

- ○ **Drug Discovery:** Generating novel molecular structures for pharmaceutical research.[21]
- ○ **Simulation and Modeling:** Creating realistic simulations for training autonomous systems and testing scenarios.
- ○ **Personalized Content:** Generating customized content tailored to individual preferences.
- **Key Generative AI Techniques:**
  - ○ **Generative Adversarial Networks (GANs):** GANs consist of two neural networks—a generator and a discriminator—that compete with each other[22] to produce realistic data.[23]
  - ○ **Variational Autoencoders (VAEs):** VAEs learn a latent representation of the data and generate new samples by

sampling from this latent space.[24]

- **Diffusion Models:** These models gradually add noise to the data and then learn to reverse the process, generating high-quality samples.[25]
- **Transformers:** Initially developed for NLP, transformers have proven highly effective in generating text, code, and even images.[26]

- **Ethical and Societal Implications:**
  - **Deepfakes and Misinformation:** The ability to generate realistic fake videos and audio raises concerns about misinformation and manipulation.[27]
  - **Copyright and Intellectual Property:** The ownership and copyright of AI-generated

content are complex legal issues.[28]

- Bias Amplification: Generative models can perpetuate and amplify biases present in the training data.[29]
- Job Displacement: The automation of creative tasks may lead to job displacement in certain industries.[30]

14.3 Quantum AI: The Next Frontier

Quantum AI represents the convergence of quantum computing and artificial intelligence, promising to unlock unprecedented computational power and revolutionize AI capabilities.[31]

- **The Synergistic Power of Quantum and AI:**

- Exponential Speedup: Quantum algorithms can solve certain problems exponentially faster than classical algorithms, accelerating AI tasks.[32]
- Enhanced Optimization: Quantum computing can tackle complex optimization problems that are intractable for classical computers, benefiting AI applications like logistics and resource management.[33]
- Quantum Machine Learning: Developing quantum algorithms for machine learning tasks, such as pattern recognition and classification.[34]
- Quantum Simulation: Simulating quantum systems for drug discovery and materials science, benefiting AI-driven research.[35]

- **Key Quantum AI Applications:**

- **Drug Discovery and Materials Science:** Simulating molecular interactions and designing new materials.
- **Financial Modeling:** Optimizing portfolios and managing risk with greater accuracy.
- **Cryptography:** Developing quantum-resistant cryptographic algorithms to protect sensitive data.[36]
- **Optimization Problems:** Solving complex combinatorial optimization problems in logistics, scheduling, and supply chain management.

- **Challenges and Future Outlook:**
  - **Hardware Development:** Building stable and scalable quantum computers remains a significant challenge.
  - **Algorithm Development:** Developing quantum algorithms

for AI tasks requires specialized expertise.[37]

- ○ **Error Correction:** Quantum computers are susceptible to noise and errors, requiring robust error correction techniques.[38]
- ○ **Hybrid Approaches:** Combining classical and quantum computing to leverage the strengths of both.[39]

14.4 AI in Specific Domains: Healthcare, Finance, and More

AI is increasingly being applied to specific domains, transforming industries and improving outcomes in areas like healthcare, finance, and beyond.[40]

- **AI in Healthcare:**

- ○ **Medical Imaging Analysis:** AI can analyze medical images (X-rays, MRIs, CT scans) to detect diseases and abnormalities with greater accuracy.[41]
- ○ **Drug Discovery and Development:** AI can accelerate the process of identifying and developing new drugs.[42]
- ○ **Personalized Medicine:** AI can analyze patient data to tailor treatments to individual needs.[43]
- ○ **Remote Patient Monitoring:** AI-powered devices can monitor patients remotely, enabling early detection of health issues.[44]
- ○ **Predictive Diagnostics:** AI can analyze patient data to predict the risk of developing certain diseases.[45]
- **AI in Finance:**

- **Fraud Detection:** AI can detect fraudulent transactions and activities in real-time.
- **Algorithmic Trading:** AI-powered algorithms can execute trades based on market data and patterns.[46]
- **Risk Management:** AI can assess and manage financial risks with greater accuracy.[47]
- **Customer Service:** AI-powered chatbots can provide 24/7 customer support.[48]
- **Financial Forecasting:** AI can analyze market data to predict future trends.[49]

- **AI in Other Domains:**
  - **Manufacturing:** AI can optimize production processes, improve quality control, and predict equipment failures.[50]
  - **Transportation:** AI can enable autonomous vehicles, optimize

traffic flow, and improve logistics.[51]

- **Agriculture:** AI can optimize crop yields, manage resources, and monitor livestock.[52]
- **Education:** AI can personalize learning experiences, provide intelligent tutoring, and automate administrative tasks.[53]
- **Retail:** AI can personalize shopping experiences, optimize inventory management, and provide targeted recommendations.[54]

14.5 The Societal Impact of Advanced AI

Advanced AI has the potential to transform society in profound ways, but it also raises significant ethical and societal considerations.[55]

- **Potential Benefits:**
  - **Increased Productivity and Efficiency:** AI can automate tasks and optimize processes, leading to greater productivity.[56]
  - **Improved Healthcare Outcomes:** AI can enhance diagnostics, personalize treatments, and accelerate drug discovery.[57]
  - **Enhanced Education and Accessibility:** AI can personalize learning experiences and provide access to knowledge for all.[58]
  - **Sustainable Development:** AI can optimize resource management, reduce waste, and mitigate climate change.[59]
  - **Scientific Discovery and Innovation:** AI can accelerate research and development in various fields.[60]
- **Potential Risks and Challenges:**

- **Job Displacement and Economic Inequality:** Automation may lead to job losses and exacerbate economic inequality.[61]
- **Bias and Discrimination:** AI systems can perpetuate and amplify biases present in the training data.[62]
- **Privacy Concerns:** The collection and analysis of personal data raise concerns about privacy and security.[63]
- **Autonomous Weapons Systems:** The development of AI-powered weapons raises ethical and security concerns.[64]

CHAPTER 15

AI and You: Continuing Your Learning Journey

The field of AI is dynamic and ever-evolving, demanding continuous learning and adaptation.[1] This chapter provides a roadmap for staying ahead, building a strong portfolio, and actively participating in the AI community.

15.1 Resources for Further Learning: Online Courses and Communities

Continuing your AI education is essential for staying relevant and expanding your expertise.[2] Numerous resources are available to support this journey.

- **Online Courses:**

- **Coursera:** Offers a wide range of AI and machine learning courses from top universities and institutions.[3]
    - Specializations in Deep Learning, Machine Learning, Natural Language Processing, and more.[4]
    - Courses from Andrew Ng, Geoffrey Hinton, and other leading experts.[5]
-
- **edX:** Provides courses from universities like MIT, Harvard, and Stanford.[6]
    - Programs in Artificial Intelligence, Computer Science, and Data Science.[7]
    - Courses on specific topics like reinforcement learning, computer vision, and robotics.[8]

-
- **Udacity:** Offers nanodegree programs designed to provide in-depth, practical skills in AI and related fields.[9]
  - Nanodegrees in Self-Driving Car Engineering, Deep Learning, and AI Product Management.[10]
  - Project-based learning with personalized feedback and career services.[11]
-
- **Fast.ai:** Provides free, practical courses on deep learning, emphasizing a top-down approach.[12]
  - Courses on deep learning for coders and natural language processing.[13]
  - Active community and supportive forums.
-

- **DeepLearning.AI:** Founded by Andrew Ng, offers courses and programs focused on deep learning and AI.[14]
  - Specializations on Coursera and standalone courses.[15]
  - Emphasis on practical skills and real-world applications.
-
- **Google Cloud Skills Boost (formerly Qwiklabs):** Offers hands-on labs and learning paths on Google Cloud's AI and machine learning services.[16]
  - Focus on practical skills and cloud-based AI tools.
-
- **Microsoft Learn:** Provides free learning paths and certifications on Microsoft's AI and machine learning technologies.[17]

- Focus on Azure AI services and tools.
  - ○
- **Online Communities and Forums:**
  - ○ **Reddit (r/MachineLearning, r/ArtificialInteligence, r/DeepLearning):** Active communities for discussions, news, and resources related to AI.[18]
  - ○ **Stack Overflow:** A platform for asking and answering programming questions, including those related to AI and machine learning.[19]
  - ○ **Kaggle Forums:** A community for data scientists and machine learning practitioners to discuss competitions, datasets, and techniques.[20]
  - ○ **LinkedIn Groups:** Join groups related to AI and

machine learning to connect with professionals and stay updated on industry trends.[21]

- ○ **Discord and Slack Communities:** Many open-source AI projects and research groups have active Discord or Slack communities for collaboration and discussion.[22]
- ○ **Medium:** A platform where many AI practitioners write about their findings, projects, and insights.

15.2 Staying Updated with the Latest AI Research

The field of AI is rapidly evolving, with new research papers and breakthroughs emerging constantly. Staying updated is crucial for staying ahead of the curve.

- **Research Papers and Preprints:**
  - **arXiv:** A repository of preprints in physics, mathematics, computer science, and other fields, including AI and machine learning.[23]
  - **NeurIPS, ICML, ICLR, CVPR, ACL:** Top conferences in AI and machine learning, publishing cutting-edge research papers.[24]
  - **Google AI Blog, DeepMind Blog, OpenAI Blog:** Blogs from leading AI research organizations, providing insights into their latest research.
  - **Papers with Code:** A website that tracks research papers and their associated code implementations.[25]
- **Newsletters and Blogs:**
  - **Import AI:** A weekly newsletter summarizing the latest AI research and developments.

- **The Batch (DeepLearning.AI):** A weekly newsletter covering AI news and insights.[26]
- **Synced:** A news and analysis platform focusing on AI and machine learning.[27]
- **AI Weekly:** A weekly newsletter highlighting the latest AI research and developments.[28]
- **Towards Data Science (Medium):** A publication on Medium featuring articles on data science, machine learning, and AI.

- **Social Media:**
  - **Twitter:** Follow leading AI researchers, organizations, and influencers to stay updated on the latest news and trends.
  - **LinkedIn:** Connect with AI professionals and follow companies and organizations in the AI space.

- **Podcasts and YouTube Channels:**
  - **Lex Fridman Podcast:** Interviews with leading AI researchers and thinkers.
  - **Talking Machines:** A podcast exploring the latest developments in machine learning.[29]
  - **Two Minute Papers:** A YouTube channel that explains complex AI research papers in a concise and accessible way.[30]
  - **Sentdex:** A YouTube channel featuring tutorials on machine learning and deep learning.[31]

15.3 Building a Portfolio of AI Projects

A strong portfolio of AI projects is essential for showcasing your skills and experience to potential employers or collaborators.

- **Project Ideas:**
  - **Image Classification:** Build a CNN model to classify images from a dataset like CIFAR-10 or ImageNet.[32]
  - **Sentiment Analysis:** Develop a sentiment analysis model to classify the sentiment of social media posts or product reviews.
  - **Chatbot Development:** Create a chatbot that can answer questions or provide information on a specific topic.
  - **Time Series Forecasting:** Build a model to predict future values in a time series dataset.
  - **Object Detection:** Develop a model to detect objects in images or videos.[33]
  - **Natural Language Generation:** Create a model that can generate text, such as stories or articles.

- Reinforcement Learning: Train an agent to play a game or solve a control problem.
- Web Application with AI: Deploy an AI model as a web service using Flask or FastAPI.[34]
- Data Visualization and Analysis: Create interactive visualizations and dashboards to explore and communicate insights from data.
- Personal Projects: Solve a problem that interests you using AI techniques.

- **Portfolio Best Practices:**
  - Choose Projects that Demonstrate Your Skills: Focus on projects that showcase your knowledge of different AI techniques and frameworks.
  - Document Your Projects Thoroughly: Provide clear explanations of your project goals, methods, and results.

- Use Version Control (Git): Track changes to your code and make it easy to collaborate.[35]
- Host Your Projects on GitHub: Make your projects publicly accessible and easy to share.
- Create a Portfolio Website: Showcase your projects and skills on a personal website.
- Contribute to Open-Source Projects: Gain experience and build your reputation by contributing to open-source AI projects.
- Participate in Kaggle Competitions: Challenge yourself and learn from other data scientists by participating in Kaggle competitions.[36]

15.4 Joining the AI Community: Contributing and Collaborating

Engaging with the AI community is a great way to learn from others, share your knowledge, and build your network.

- **Ways to Contribute:**
    - **Answer Questions on Forums and Communities:** Help others by answering questions on Stack Overflow, Reddit, and other platforms.
    - **Write Blog Posts or Tutorials:** Share your knowledge and insights by writing blog posts or creating tutorials on AI topics.
    - **Give Talks or Presentations:** Present your work at conferences, meetups, or workshops.

- o **Mentor Others:** Share your experience and knowledge by mentoring aspiring AI practitioners.
- o **Contribute to Open-Source Projects:** Help improve open-source AI projects by contributing code, documentation, or bug fixes.[37]
- o **Organize Meetups or Workshops:** Create opportunities for others to learn and connect by organizing AI-related events.
- **Benefits of Collaboration:**
  - o **Learn from Others:** Gain new perspectives and insights by collaborating with other AI practitioners.
  - o **Expand Your Network:** Connect with professionals and researchers in the AI field.
  - o **Build Your Reputation:** Establish yourself as a

knowledgeable and active member of the AI community.

- ○ **Contribute to Meaningful Projects:** Work on projects that have a positive impact on society.
- ○ **Gain Access to New Opportunities:** Collaboration can lead to new job opportunities, research collaborations, and other professional opportunities.

By embracing continuous learning, building a strong portfolio, and actively participating in the AI community, you can embark on a fulfilling and impactful career in the field of Artificial Intelligence.

Conclusion: The Power of AI: Transforming the World Around Us

As we conclude this comprehensive exploration of Artificial Intelligence, it's essential to reflect on the profound impact AI has already had and the even greater potential it holds for the future. AI is not merely a technological advancement; it's a paradigm shift that is reshaping industries, redefining human-machine interactions, and ultimately, transforming the world around us.[1]

Recap of Key Concepts and Skills

Throughout this journey, we've delved into the core principles of AI, spanning from foundational machine learning algorithms to cutting-edge deep learning architectures. We've explored:

- **Supervised Learning:** Understanding how to build models that learn from labeled data, including regression for predicting continuous values and classification for predicting categorical labels.[2]
- **Unsupervised Learning:** Discovering hidden patterns and structures in unlabeled data through clustering and dimensionality reduction.[3]
- **Neural Networks and Deep Learning:** Building complex models inspired by the human brain, capable of tackling intricate tasks like image recognition and natural language processing.[4]
- **Natural Language Processing (NLP):** Empowering machines to understand and generate human language, enabling applications like sentiment analysis and chatbots.[5]
- **Reinforcement Learning (RL):** Training agents to learn through

interaction with an environment, optimizing decision-making in dynamic situations.[6]

- **Practical Implementation:** Gaining hands-on experience by building AI applications in Python using libraries like Scikit-learn, TensorFlow, and PyTorch.
- **Deployment:** Learning how to serialize models, deploy them as web services or in the cloud, and maintain them in production environments.[7]
- **Emerging Trends:** Exploring the future of AI through XAI, Generative AI, Quantum AI, and AI in specific domains.

These concepts and skills form the bedrock of AI expertise, providing a solid foundation for building innovative and impactful applications.[8]

The Importance of Ethical AI Development

The power of AI comes with significant responsibility. As AI systems become more pervasive, it's crucial to prioritize ethical considerations in their development and deployment.

- **Fairness and Bias:** AI models can perpetuate and amplify biases present in the training data, leading to discriminatory outcomes.[9] We must strive to develop fair and equitable AI systems that treat all individuals with respect.
- **Transparency and Accountability:** The "black box" nature of some AI models can make it difficult to understand their decision-making processes.[10] Explainable AI (XAI) is essential for

building trust and ensuring accountability.[11]

- **Privacy and Security:** AI systems often collect and process vast amounts of personal data, raising concerns about privacy and security.[12] Robust security measures and ethical data handling practices are paramount.
- **Social Impact:** AI has the potential to disrupt industries and displace jobs.[13] We must consider the broader social impact of AI technologies and work to mitigate any negative consequences.
- **Human Control:** It's crucial to maintain human control over AI systems, ensuring that they are used for the benefit of humanity.[14]
- **Responsible Innovation:** We must foster a culture of responsible innovation, where ethical considerations are integrated into every stage of AI development.[15]

- **Regulation and Governance:** Developing appropriate regulations and governance frameworks is essential for guiding the responsible development and deployment of AI.[16]

Encouraging Continued Exploration and Innovation

The field of AI is characterized by rapid innovation and continuous learning.[17] We encourage you to embrace this spirit of exploration and contribute to the advancement of AI.

- **Stay Curious:** Cultivate a lifelong learning mindset, staying updated on the latest research and developments in AI.[18]
- **Experiment and Innovate:** Don't be afraid to experiment with new techniques and approaches. Push the boundaries of what's possible with AI.

- **Build a Portfolio:** Develop a strong portfolio of AI projects to showcase your skills and experience.
- **Contribute to the Community:** Share your knowledge and expertise by contributing to open-source projects, writing blog posts, or participating in online forums.
- **Collaborate and Network:** Connect with other AI practitioners and researchers to learn from each other and collaborate on impactful projects.
- **Embrace Interdisciplinary Thinking:** AI intersects with various disciplines, from ethics and law to psychology and sociology.[19] Embrace interdisciplinary thinking to develop holistic solutions.
- **Focus on Impact:** Prioritize projects that have a positive impact on society and address real-world challenges.
- **Think Critically:** Approach AI with a critical mindset, questioning

assumptions and challenging conventional wisdom.

- **Seek Mentorship:** Find mentors who can guide you on your AI journey and provide valuable insights.
- **Never Stop Learning:** The field of AI is constantly evolving, so continuous learning is essential for staying ahead.[20]

The future of AI is in your hands. By embracing ethical development, fostering innovation, and engaging with the AI community, you can play a vital role in shaping a future where AI benefits all of humanity. Let us continue to explore, innovate, and build a world where the power of AI is harnessed for the greater good.

Appendix

This appendix serves as a valuable resource for navigating the practical aspects of AI development and deepening your understanding of key concepts.

Appendix A: Python Libraries Installation Guide

Setting up a robust Python environment is crucial for any AI project. Let's explore the process in more detail, including best practices and troubleshooting tips.

- **Virtual Environments: The Cornerstone of Dependency Management**
  - Virtual environments create isolated Python environments, preventing conflicts between project dependencies.[1]
  - **Why Use Virtual Environments?**

- **Dependency Isolation:** Different projects may require different versions of the same library.[2] Virtual environments allow you to manage these dependencies independently.[3]
- **Reproducibility:** Virtual environments ensure that your project can be replicated on any machine with the same dependencies.[4]
- **Cleanliness:** They keep your system's global Python installation clean and organized.[5]

- **Advanced Virtual Environment Management:**
  - **venv vs. conda:** While venv is part of the standard Python library, conda (from Anaconda) is

another popular option. Conda excels at managing non-Python dependencies and creating cross-platform environments.

- **Using** virtualenvwrapper**:** For enhanced virtual environment management, consider virtualenvwrapper. It provides convenient commands for creating, activating, and managing virtual environments.[6]

- **pip: Your Package Management Powerhouse**
  - pip is the primary tool for installing and managing Python packages.
  - **Advanced pip Usage:**
    - **Installing Specific Versions:** pip install <library_name>==<versio

n_number> (e.g., pip install tensorflow==2.9.0).

- **Installing from Local Files:** pip install <path_to_wheel_or_tarball>.

- **Using Requirements Files:** requirements.txt is crucial for reproducibility. It lists all project dependencies and their versions.

- **Understanding pip cache:** Pip maintains a cache of downloaded packages.[7] You can clear the cache using pip cache purge.

- **Using pip check:** To verify that installed dependencies have compatible requirements.[8]

- **Key Libraries: A Deep Dive**

- TensorFlow/Keras vs. PyTorch: Both are powerful deep learning frameworks.
  - **TensorFlow/Keras:** Known for its production-ready deployment tools and robust ecosystem.[9]
  - **PyTorch:** Favored for its dynamic computation graph and ease of use in research.[10]
- **Scikit-learn: The Swiss Army Knife of ML:** Essential for traditional ML tasks.
  - Explore its preprocessing tools, various model implementations, and evaluation metrics.
- **Pandas: Data Wrangling Wizardry:** Essential for data manipulation.
  - Learn about its powerful data structures

(DataFrame and Series) and data cleaning functions.

- NLTK vs. spaCy: Both are NLP libraries.
    - **NLTK:** A comprehensive toolkit with a wide range of algorithms and resources.[11]
    - **spaCy:** Known for its speed and efficiency, making it suitable for production environments.[12]
- **Transformers (Hugging Face):** Provides access to state-of-the-art pretrained models.[13]
    - Explore its models for various NLP tasks, including text classification, question answering, and text generation.

- o
  - **OpenCV:** Computer vision library.[14]
    - For image and video processing.
  - o
  - **Seaborn/Plotly:** Advanced data visualization.
    - Seaborn, great for statistical visualization.[15]
    - Plotly, great for interactive visualization.[16]
- **Troubleshooting Installation Issues:**
  - **"Permission denied" errors:** Use sudo (macOS/Linux) or run the command prompt as administrator (Windows).
  - **"Could not build wheels" errors:** Ensure you have the necessary build tools installed (e.g., build-essential on Linux).

- "DLL load failed" errors (Windows): Ensure you have the correct Visual C++ Redistributable installed.
- "Cuda out of memory" errors: reduce batch size, or move to a larger GPU.[17]

Appendix B: Glossary of AI Terms

Let's expand on the glossary, providing more context and examples.

- **Activation Function:**
  - A function applied to the output of a neuron, introducing non-linearity to the network.[18]
  - Examples: ReLU, sigmoid, tanh.
- **Artificial Neural Network (ANN):**

- A computational model inspired by the structure and function of the human brain.
- Consists of interconnected nodes (neurons) organized in layers.[19]
- **Bias-Variance Tradeoff:**
  - A fundamental concept in machine learning that describes the tradeoff between bias (underfitting) and variance (overfitting).
- **Cost Function (Loss Function):**
  - A function that measures the error between predicted and actual values.
  - Used to optimize model parameters.
- **Cross-Validation:**
  - A technique for evaluating model performance by partitioning the data into multiple folds.
  - Helps to prevent overfitting.

- **Dimensionality Reduction:**
  - A technique for reducing the number of features in a dataset while preserving essential information.
  - Examples: PCA, t-SNE.
- **Epoch:**
  - One complete pass through the entire training dataset during model training.
- **Hyperparameter:**
  - A parameter that is set before training a model.
  - Examples: learning rate, number of layers.
- **Kernel Trick:**
  - A technique used in SVMs to map data into a higher-dimensional space, enabling non-linear classification.
- **Natural Language Understanding (NLU):**

- A subfield of NLP that focuses on understanding the meaning of human language.[20]
- **Regularization:**
  - A technique used to prevent overfitting by adding a penalty term to the loss function.
  - Examples: L1, L2.
- **Transfer Learning:**
  - A technique that involves using a pre-trained model as a starting point for a new task.
- **Transformer Network:**
  - A neural network architecture that relies heavily on attention mechanisms, excelling at sequence to sequence tasks, such as translation, and text summarization.[21]
- **Reinforcement Learning Agent:**
  - An entity that learns to make decisions by interacting with an environment, aiming to maximize cumulative reward.

- **Generative Adversarial Network (GAN):**
  - A generative model consisting of two neural networks, a generator and a discriminator, that compete with each other.[22]
- **Explainable AI (XAI):**
  - Techniques and methods that enable humans to understand and interpret AI models.

Appendix C: Common AI Datasets and Resources

Let's explore datasets and resources in more detail, including their characteristics and applications.

- **Text Datasets (Continued):**
  - **GLUE (General Language Understanding Evaluation benchmark):**[2]

- A collection of diverse natural language understanding tasks.[3]
- Used to evaluate the performance of NLP models.
- Includes tasks like sentiment analysis, question answering, and textual entailment.[4]

-
- **Common Crawl:**
  - A massive dataset of web pages.[5]
  - Used for training large language models and other NLP tasks.
  - Requires significant processing and filtering.
- **The Pile:**
  - A large, diverse dataset of text from various sources.[6]

- Designed to train general-purpose language models.[7]
- Includes data from books, code, and websites.[8]
- **Other Datasets:**
  - **UCI Machine Learning Repository:**
    - A classic repository of diverse datasets for machine learning.[9]
    - Includes datasets for classification, regression, and clustering.[10]
    - A valuable resource for beginners.
  - **Kaggle Datasets:**
    - A platform for data science competitions and datasets.[11]
    - Offers a wide range of datasets for various AI tasks.[12]

- Provides a community for sharing and discussing data.
- **Google Dataset Search:**
  - A search engine for datasets.[13]
  - Helps you find datasets from various sources.[14]
  - Useful for discovering datasets relevant to your specific needs.
- **OpenML:**
  - An open machine learning platform and repository.[15]
  - Provides a collaborative environment for sharing datasets and experiments.[16]
  - Focuses on reproducibility and open science.
- **NASA C-MAPSS:**
  - Computational Model for Aero-Propulsion System Simulation.

- Used for predictive maintenance.
- Contains sensor data from simulated aircraft engines.

- **Resources:**
  - **Papers with Code:**
    - A website that tracks research papers and their associated code implementations.
    - Helps you find code for implementing state-of-the-art AI models.
    - A valuable resource for staying updated on the latest research.
  - **arXiv:**
    - A repository of preprints in AI and machine learning.
    - Provides access to cutting-edge research before it is published in journals.

- Essential for staying informed about the latest advancements.
- **DeepLearning.AI:**
  - Educational resources and courses on deep learning.
  - Offers high-quality content from leading experts.
  - A great place to learn about deep learning concepts and techniques.
- **Google AI Blog:**
  - Insights into Google's AI research and projects.
  - Provides updates on Google's AI initiatives and breakthroughs.
  - A valuable source of information on Google's AI efforts.
- **OpenAI Blog:**
  - Updates on OpenAI's research and projects.

- Provides insights into OpenAI's work on cutting-edge AI technologies.
- A must-read for staying informed about OpenAI's advancements.

Appendix D: Troubleshooting Common Python and AI Errors

- **ModuleNotFoundError: No module named '...'**
  - **Cause:** The required Python library is not installed in your environment.
  - **Solution:**
    - Use pip install <module_name> to install the missing library.

- Ensure you are working in the correct virtual environment.
- If using conda, use conda install <module_name>.

- **ValueError: could not convert string to float: '...'**
  - **Cause:** Your code is attempting to convert a string that cannot be interpreted as a number to a float.
  - **Solution:**
    - Inspect the data to identify the problematic string.
    - Use error handling (e.g., try-except blocks) to handle invalid data.
    - Preprocess the data to clean or correct invalid values.
- **TypeError: unsupported operand type(s) for +: 'int' and 'str'**

- **Cause:** You are trying to perform an operation (e.g., addition) on incompatible data types.
- **Solution:**
  - Check the data types of the variables involved in the operation.
  - Use type conversion functions (e.g., int(), float(), str()) to ensure compatible types.
  - Ensure that the variables are holding the types of data that your code expects.

- **IndexError: list index out of range**
  - **Cause:** Your code is trying to access an element of a list using an index that is outside the valid range.
  - **Solution:**

- Check the length of the list and the index you are using.
- Use conditional statements to prevent accessing invalid indices.
- Use list comprehensions or other techniques to create lists with the correct size.

- **MemoryError:**
  - **Cause:** Your program is consuming more memory than is available.
  - **Solution:**
    - Reduce the size of the data being processed.
    - Use more efficient data structures or algorithms.
    - Process data in smaller batches.
    - If possible, move to a machine with more RAM.
- **CUDA out of memory:**

- **Cause:** Your deep learning model is exceeding the available GPU memory.
- **Solution:**
  - Reduce the batch size.
  - Use mixed-precision training.
  - Use gradient accumulation.
  - Move to a GPU with more memory.
  - Close other applications that are using GPU resources.

- **Version Mismatch:**
  - **Cause:** Incompatibilities between library versions.
  - **Solution:**
    - Use virtual environments to isolate project dependencies.
    - Carefully read the documentation for the libraries you are using.

- Upgrade or downgrade libraries to compatible versions using pip.
- Check for dependency conflicts using pip check.
- **SyntaxError: invalid syntax**
  - **Cause:** Problem with the python code syntax.
  - **Solution:**
    - Carefully check the code for typos.
    - Verify that all parenthesis, brackets, and quotation marks are correctly matched.
    - Ensure that colons are present at the end of control flow statements(if, for, while, def, class).
    - Use a code editor that highlights syntax errors.

Absolutely. Let's provide an extensive and comprehensive exploration of the mathematical foundations of key AI algorithms, focusing on clarity, depth, and educational value.

Appendix E: Mathematical Foundations of Key Algorithms

Understanding the mathematical underpinnings of AI algorithms is crucial for building a solid foundation in the field. This section delves into the mathematical concepts behind some of the most fundamental algorithms, providing a comprehensive and detailed explanation.

1. Linear Regression

Linear regression aims to model the relationship between a dependent variable (y) and one or more independent variables (x)[1] using a linear equation.[2]

- **Mathematical Model:**

- Simple Linear Regression (one independent variable): $y = \beta_0 + \beta_1 x + \varepsilon$
- Multiple Linear Regression (multiple independent variables): $y = \beta_0 + \beta_1 x_1 + \beta_2 x_2 + \dots + \beta_\square x_\square + \varepsilon$
- Where:
  - y is the dependent variable.
  - x are the independent variables.
  - β_0 is the y-intercept.
  - β_i are the coefficients (slopes) for each independent variable.
  - ε is the error term (residuals).
- **Objective:**
  - To find the values of β_0 and β_i that minimize the difference between the predicted values ($\hat{y}$) and the actual values (y).
- **Loss Function:**

- Mean Squared Error (MSE): $MSE = 1/n \, \Sigma(y_i - \hat{y}_i)^2$
- Where:
    - n is the number of data points.
    - y_i is the actual value.
    - $\hat{y}_i$ is the predicted value.
- **Optimization:**
    - **Ordinary Least Squares (OLS):** A closed-form solution to find the optimal coefficients.[3]
        - $\beta = (X^T X)^{-1} X^T y$
        - Where:
            - β is the vector of coefficients.
            - X is the matrix of independent variables.
            - y is the vector of dependent variables.
    -
    - **Gradient Descent:** An iterative optimization algorithm that updates the coefficients in

the direction of the negative gradient of the loss function.[4]

- $\beta_\square = \beta_\square - \alpha \, \partial(MSE)/\partial\beta_\square$
- Where:
    - α is the learning rate.
    - $\partial(MSE)/\partial\beta_\square$ is the partial derivative of the MSE with respect to $\beta_\square$.

    ○

- **Key Concepts:**
    - Matrix algebra (matrix multiplication, transpose, inverse).
    - Calculus (partial derivatives, gradient).[5]
    - Statistical concepts (residuals, variance).

2. Logistic Regression

Logistic regression is a classification algorithm used to predict the probability of a binary outcome.[67]

- **Mathematical Model:**
  - $p(y=1) = 1 / (1 + e^{\wedge}(-z))$ (sigmoid function)
  - Where:
    - $p(y=1)$ is the probability of the outcome being 1.
    - $z = \beta_0 + \beta_1 x_1 + \beta_2 x_2 + ... + \beta_\square x_\square$ (linear combination of features).
- **Objective:**
  - To find the values of β_0 and β_i that maximize the likelihood of observing the given data.
- **Loss Function:**
  - Cross-Entropy Loss (Log Loss):
    - $L(y, p) = -1/n \; \Sigma[y_i \log(p_i) + (1 - y_i) \log(1 - p_i)]$
    - Where:
      - y_i is the actual label (0 or 1).

- p_i is the predicted probability.
- **Optimization:**
  - **Maximum Likelihood Estimation (MLE):** A statistical method to find the parameters that maximize the likelihood function.[8]
  - **Gradient Descent:** Used to minimize the cross-entropy loss.
    - $\beta\square = \beta\square - \alpha\, \partial(L)/\partial\beta\square$
- **Key Concepts:**
  - Sigmoid function (logistic function).[9]
  - Maximum likelihood estimation.
  - Cross-entropy loss.
  - Calculus (derivatives).

3. K-Means Clustering

K-means clustering is an unsupervised learning algorithm used to partition data points into k clusters.[10]

- **Objective:**
  - To minimize the within-cluster sum of squared distances (WCSS).
- **Mathematical Formulation:**
  - Objective Function: $\text{WCSS} = \Sigma\,\Sigma\,||x_i - \mu_\square||^2$
  - Where:
    - x_i is a data point.
    - $\mu_\square$ is the centroid of cluster j.
    - $||x_i - \mu_\square||$ is the Euclidean distance between x_i and $\mu_\square$.
- **Algorithm:**
  - **Initialization:** Randomly initialize k cluster centroids.
  - **Assignment:** Assign each data point to the cluster with the nearest centroid.
  - **Update:** Recalculate the centroids as the mean of the data points assigned to each cluster.

- Iteration: Repeat steps 2 and 3 until convergence.[11]
- **Key Concepts:**
    - Euclidean distance.
    - Centroid calculation (mean).
    - Iterative optimization.

4. Convolutional Neural Networks (CNNs)

CNNs are deep learning models designed for image processing, using convolution operations to learn hierarchical features.[12]

- **Convolution Operation:**
    - $S(i, j) = (I * K)(i, j) = \Sigma \Sigma I(m, n) K(i - m, j - n)$
    - Where:
        - I is the input image.
        - K is the kernel (filter).
        - S is the feature map.
- **Pooling Operation:**

- Reduces the spatial dimensions of feature maps.
- **Max Pooling:** Selects the maximum value in a pooling window.
- **Average Pooling:** Calculates the average value in a pooling window.

- **Activation Functions:**
  - Introduce non-linearity to the network.
  - **ReLU (Rectified Linear Unit):** $f(x) = \max(0, x)$
  - **Sigmoid:** $f(x) = 1 / (1 + e^{\wedge}(-x))$
  - **Tanh (Hyperbolic Tangent):** $f(x) = (e^{\wedge}x - e^{\wedge}(-x)) / (e^{\wedge}x + e^{\wedge}(-x))$

- **Loss Function:**
  - Categorical Cross-Entropy (for classification).
  - Mean Squared Error (for regression).

- **Optimization:**

- Backpropagation (using gradient descent).[13]
- **Key Concepts:**
    - Convolution operation.
    - Pooling operation.
    - Activation functions.
    - Backpropagation.
    - Calculus (derivatives, chain rule).[14]

5. Recurrent Neural Networks (RNNs)

RNNs are deep learning models designed for sequential data processing, using recurrent connections to maintain memory.[15]

- **Recurrent Cell:**
    - $h_t = f(Wx_t + Uh_{t-1} + b)$
    - Where:
        - h_t is the hidden state at time t.
        - x_t is the input at time t.

- h_{t-1} is the hidden state at time t-1.
- W, U, and b are weights and biases.
- f is an activation function.

- **Loss Function:**
  - Cross-Entropy Loss (for classification).
  - Mean Squared Error (for regression).
- **Optimization:**
  - Backpropagation Through Time (BPTT).
- **Key Concepts:**
  - Recurrent connections.
  - Hidden states.
  - Backpropagation Through Time.
  - Calculus (derivatives, chain rule).[16]

6. Principal Component Analysis (PCA)

PCA is a dimensionality reduction technique that finds the principal components of a dataset.[17]

- **Objective:**
    - To find the orthogonal directions (principal components) that capture the maximum variance in the data.[18]
- **Algorithm:**
    - **Standardization:** Standardize the data to have zero mean and unit variance.
    - **Covariance Matrix:** Calculate the covariance matrix of the standardized data.
    - **Eigenvalues and Eigenvectors:** Calculate the eigenvalues and eigenvectors of the covariance matrix.
    - **Principal Components:** Select the eigenvectors corresponding to the largest eigenvalues.

- ○ **Transformation:** Transform the data into the lower-dimensional space using the selected eigenvectors.
- • **Key Concepts:**
  - ○ Covariance matrix.
  - ○ Eigenvalues
  - ○ **Eigenvectors:** Vectors that, when multiplied by a matrix, result in a scaled version of themselves. They represent the directions of maximum variance in the data.
  - ○ **Eigenvalues:** Scalars that represent the magnitude of the variance captured by each eigenvector. Larger eigenvalues correspond to more significant principal components.
  - ○ **Variance:** A statistical measure of the spread of data. PCA aims to maximize the variance captured by the principal components.

- **Orthogonality:** Principal components are orthogonal (perpendicular) to each other, meaning they are uncorrelated.
- **Dimensionality Reduction:** By selecting a subset of principal components, we can reduce the dimensionality of the data while retaining most of its variance.

7. Support Vector Machines (SVMs)

SVMs are powerful supervised learning algorithms used for classification and regression.

- **Objective:**
  - To find the hyperplane that maximally separates data points of different classes.
- **Mathematical Formulation:**
  - **Hyperplane Equation:** $w^Tx + b = 0$

- Where:
  - w is the weight vector (normal to the hyperplane).
  - x is the input vector.
  - b is the bias term.
- **Margin:** The distance between the hyperplane and the nearest data points (support vectors).
- **Optimization:**
  - Minimize $||w||^2$ subject to $y_i(w^Tx_i + b) \geq 1$ (for classification).
  - Where:
    - y_i is the label of the i-th data point.
- **Kernel Trick:**
  - Maps data into a higher-dimensional space to handle non-linear separation.
  - Examples: linear, polynomial, radial basis function (RBF).

- **Key Concepts:**
    - Hyperplane.
    - Margin maximization.
    - Support vectors.
    - Kernel functions.
    - Quadratic programming (for optimization).

8. Naive Bayes

Naive Bayes is a probabilistic classification algorithm based on Bayes' theorem with a "naive" independence assumption.

- **Bayes' Theorem:**
    - $P(A|B) = P(B|A) \, P(A) / P(B)$
    - Where:
        - $P(A|B)$ is the posterior probability of A given B.
        - $P(B|A)$ is the likelihood of B given A.
        - $P(A)$ is the prior probability of A.

- **P(B)** is the[1] prior probability of B.
- **Naive Assumption:**
  - Assumes that features are conditionally independent given the class label.
  - $P(x_1, x_2, ..., x_\square|y) = P(x_1|y) P(x_2|y) ... P(x_\square|y)$
- **Classification:**
  - $y = \text{argmax } P(y|x_1, x_2, ..., x_\square)$
  - Using Bayes' theorem and the naive assumption.
- **Key Concepts:**
  - Bayes' theorem.
  - Conditional probability.
  - Independence assumption.
  - Probability distributions (Gaussian, Bernoulli, Multinomial).

9. Decision Trees

Decision trees are tree-like structures used for classification and regression.

- **Objective:**
  - To partition the data space into regions based on feature values.
- **Algorithm:**
  - Recursive partitioning of the data based on feature splits.
  - Splits are chosen to maximize information gain or minimize impurity (e.g., Gini impurity, entropy).
- **Information Gain:**
  - Measures the reduction in entropy after a split.
  - $IG(S, A) = Entropy(S) - \Sigma\, (|S_v| / |S|)\, Entropy(S_v)$
    - Where S is the data set, A is an attribute, and Sv is the subset of S where attribute A has value v.
- **Gini Impurity:**

- Measures the probability of misclassifying a randomly chosen element if it were randomly labeled according to the distribution of labels in the subset.[2]
- $Gini(S) = 1 - \Sigma p_i^2$
  - Where pi is the proportion of elements in set S that are in class i.

- **Key Concepts:**
  - Tree structure.
  - Information gain.
  - Gini impurity.
  - Entropy.
  - Recursive partitioning.

10. Gradient Boosting

Gradient boosting is an ensemble learning technique that combines multiple weak learners (e.g., decision trees) to create a strong learner.

- **Algorithm:**
  - Iteratively trains weak learners, each focusing on the errors made by the previous learners.
  - Uses gradient descent to minimize a loss function.
- **Loss Function:**
  - Can be any differentiable loss function (e.g., MSE, cross-entropy).
- **Key Concepts:**
  - Ensemble learning.
  - Weak learners.
  - Gradient descent.
  - Additive modeling.

These mathematical foundations provide a deeper understanding of how AI algorithms work. By grasping these concepts, you can build a stronger foundation for developing and applying AI solutions.

www.ingramcontent.com/pod-product-compliance
Lightning Source LLC
La Vergne TN
LVHW051428050326
832903LV00030BD/2976